ONEplus Therapy

By the same author
in the Single-Session Therapy series:

Single-Session Therapy @ Onlinevents
(Onlinevents Publications, 2021)

'I Wish You a Healthy Christmas':
Single-Session Therapy in Action
(Onlinevents Publications, 2022)

Single-Session Therapy and Regret
(Onlinevents Publications, 2023)

ONEplus Therapy

Help at the Point of Need

Windy Dryden

Onlinevents Publications

First edition published by Onlinevents Publications

Copyright (c) 2023 Windy Dryden and Onlinevents Publications

Windy Dryden
136 Montagu Mansions, London W1U 6LQ

Onlinevents Publications
38 Bates Street, Sheffield, S10 1NQ
www.onlinevents.co.uk
help@onlinevents.co.uk

First edition 2023

ISBN: 978-1-914938-27-6

Contents

Appendices

For Moshe Talmon

1

Introduction

I completed my initial therapy training in 1975. It was a course in what was known then as 'client-centred therapy'.[1] The assumptions on which this training was based were that (a) the therapist's role was to facilitate the development of a therapeutic relationship with the client based on the client's experience of the therapist as empathic, genuine and respectful, and (b) the development of this relationship took time. The idea that productive therapeutic work could take place in a single session where the client experiences this brief encounter with a therapist to be helpful so that they do not need to return for further help was never even entertained, let alone considered. In one sense, this was understandable. The first article, with 'single-session psychotherapy' in the title, was only published in 1975, the year my training finished (Spoerl, 1975). In another sense, as trainees on placement, we all encountered clients who only attended one session. In supervision, the understanding generally was that we had failed to develop the beginnings of the facilitative relationship, which was our primary task to initiate. In other words, it was our fault when a client only came once!

Almost fifty years later, even though single-session therapy is known as a form of therapy delivery, it is still barely considered in professional training programmes. Therapists currently trained are poorly equipped to deal with a sizeable number of clients looking to be helped quickly by the professionals they consult. This is one of the reasons why I have authored this book.

---

[1] Now known as 'person centred therapy'.

7

In this introductory chapter, I will mention some of the milestones that mark the path towards the development of single-session therapy.

It All Began with Freud

While the term 'single-session therapy' has been around for about fifty years (see Spoerl, 1975), the phenomenon of helping people in a single visit has been around for much longer. Indeed, there are two published cases where Sigmund Freud, the father of psychoanalysis (hardly a brief treatment!), helped individuals with their problems in one meeting.

Freud's Single Session with Aurelia Öhm-Kronich ('Katharina')

In 1893, Freud was asked to informally see Aurelia, an 18-year-old innkeeper's daughter, when he was on holiday in Austria. She complained of a suffocating feeling, accompanied by the vision of a terrifying face. These feelings started after she had witnessed her uncle[2] having sex with a maid. Freud helped Aurelia to trace these feelings back to times when her 'uncle' made sexual advances to her and, latterly, when he showed her that he was angry with her. Aurelia's anxiety symptoms diminished after being helped to make sense of her feelings in a single session (Freud & Breuer, 1895).

Freud's Single Session with Gustav Mahler

Gustav Mahler, the famous composer, contacted Sigmund Freud for an appointment even though he was aware that Freud was on vacation. When they eventually met, Freud conducted a four-hour 'walking consultation' in the Dutch university town of

---

[2] It transpired that this 'uncle' was Aurelia's father.

Leiden on 26 August 1910. In a paper on this 'treatment', Kuehn (1965: 358) notes that 'Freud's diagnosis and reassurance seemed to be very helpful. At least no more was heard from the manifest problem[3] throughout the remaining eight months of Mahler's life.'

Despite these experiences, Freud did not take the learnings from his single-session successes back to his long-term therapy practice in Vienna. If he had, the development of psychotherapy might have been very different.

'Gloria'

One of the most memorable experiences of my initial therapy training was watching what has come to be known as the 'Gloria' films (Shostrom, 1965). In this project, a client known as Gloria had three 30-minute sessions each with the founder of a well-known therapy approach: Carl Rogers (the founder of what is now known as Person Centred Therapy), Fritz Perls (the founder of Gestalt Therapy) and Albert Ellis (the founder of what is now known as Rational Emotive Behaviour Therapy). When I first saw them, it did not occur to me that these were examples of single-session therapy (SST), but that was precisely what they were: filmed therapy demonstrations of single-session conversations, each showing that a person could be helped quickly in different ways. This became one of the foundations of current SST. There is no one way of practising single-session therapy, and therapists from a broad range of different therapy approaches can practise this form of therapy delivery.

Watching the 'Gloria' films also taught me that seeing therapists practise therapy with clients discussing real problems rather than in role-played scenarios is vital to one's education as a therapist. Consequently, whenever I run a training programme or give a workshop, I do one or two live demonstrations with members of the audience who are prepared to discuss a current issue with me with which they are struggling. This is followed

---

[3] Of not being able to have sexual relations with his wife.

by a Q&A session where audience members question my client and me about our experiences.

Let's Not Forget Bernard Bloom (1923–2020)

People usually point to the publication of Moshe Talmon's (1990) book as a critical event in the development of SST, and indeed, this is the case. However, the work of Bernard Bloom is equally significant. Bloom (1981) was one of the first to offer a coherent, focused approach to SST. His approach was informed by psychodynamic therapy, and therapy sessions lasted between 60 and 80 minutes (Bloom, 1992). Like most approaches to SST that came after, Bloom stressed to his SST clients that more sessions would be provided if required.

In his early publication, Bloom (1981) outlined several therapeutic factors that characterised his focused approach to SST. These were:

- identify a focal problem;
- do not underestimate the patient's strengths;
- be prudently active;
- explore, then present interpretations tentatively;
- encourage the expression of affect;
- use the interview to start a problem-solving process;
- keep track of time;
- do not be overambitious
- keep factual questions to a minimum;
- do not be overly concerned about the precipitating event;
- avoid detours;
- do not overestimate a client's self-awareness (i.e. don't ignore stating the obvious).

In his later work, Bloom (1992) added the following principles:

- help mobilise social supports;
- educate when patients appear to lack information;
- build-in a follow-up plan.

Many of Bloom's principles are present in others' later contributions to SST (including my own), yet, in my view, his contributions have not been sufficiently well recognised. Referring to his publications in this volume is my way of honouring him and his work.

Moshe Goes to Hayward

In the mid-1980s, Moshe Talmon, an Israeli psychologist, left his long-term therapy private practice in his homeland to go and work at Kaiser Permanente, a public mental health clinic in Hayward, Northern California. After a while, he audited his work and was shocked to find that 200 of his cases attended one session when he expected them to attend more. When he asked his North American colleagues about this, they confirmed that it was common, that their clientele was not easy to engage, and that they were not very psychologically minded. Talmon was unsatisfied with this explanation, so he contacted these clients to discover the reasons for their non-attendance. He found that 78% said they were pleased with the session they had because it had helped them address their problems and did not require further help at that time. Talmon (1990) referred to this phenomenon as unplanned single-session therapy (SST).

... And meets Michael and Robert

After this, Talmon teamed up with two colleagues at Kaiser Permanente, Michael Hoyt and Robert Rosenbaum. They decided to collaborate on a study of the effects of planned single-session therapy (SST) on 60 clients, where they served as the study's therapists. As we have seen, planned SST sets out to work with the client to help them to achieve their stated wants from the session while agreeing that further help is available if needed. Fifty-eight of the study's 60 clients concluded the study, and 58.6% of this group considered a single session sufficient (Hoyt, Rosenbaum & Talmon, 1992).

Open Access, Walk-in Services

Single-session therapy can be offered by appointment or through open access, walk-in services. Walk-in services have been concisely described thus: 'walk-in therapy enables clients to meet with a mental health professional at their moment of choosing. There is no red tape, no triage, no intake process, no waiting list, and no wait. There is no formal assessment, no formal diagnostic process, just one hour of therapy focused on clients' stated wants' (Slive, McElheran & Lawson, 2008: 6). Through the pioneering efforts of Arnie Slive and Monte Bobele (2011), many people in the United States, Canada and Australia, in particular, have benefitted from receiving immediate psychological help when they want it. While these services are an integral part of the single-session therapy movement, I will not feature this work here as it is outside my range of experience.

Single-Session Therapy Develops

Due to the work of the people I have mentioned in this introductory chapter, single-session therapy has developed to the point that there are now regular international symposia. The first one took place in Melbourne, Australia, in 2012 (Hoyt & Talmon, 2014), the second took place in Banff, Canada, in 2016 (Hoyt, Bobele, Young & Talmon, 2018), and the third was held again in Melbourne in 2019 (Hoyt, Young & Rycroft, 2021). The next international symposium will take place in Rome in November 2023. The edited books that these international symposia spawned show the wide range of developments that have taken place in the field of SST in the last 35 years.

While there are too many such developments to mention

here, I would like to reference three that I consider especially significant. In this respect, I want to mention the work of:

- Jessica Schleider and her colleagues at Stony Brook University for their work in developing and researching single-session digital interventions for young people (e.g., Schleider, Dobias, Sung & Mullarkey, 2020).

- Jeff Young, Pam Rycroft and their colleagues at the Bouverie Centre, La Trobe University, for their work in developing family therapy-based SST, online SST training and a single-session approach to supervision (e.g., Rycroft & Young, 2021)

- Martin Söderquist and his colleagues in Sweden for their work in developing single-session counselling with couples (e.g., Söderquist, 2023)

What's in a Name?

In this final section of this introductory chapter, I will consider the issues one faces when deciding what to call the mode of therapy delivery, which is the book's focus. I will review the two significant terms currently used: Single-Session Therapy (SST) and One-At-A-Time Therapy (OAATT) and explain my reservations about them. Then I will explain why I prefer the term ONEplus Therapy.

Single-Session Therapy

Whenever I give a training workshop on single-session therapy, I stress that the purpose of SST is for the therapist and client to work together to see if they can help the client meet their stated wants from the session while acknowledging that more help is available to the client if requested. However, people continue to hear that the nature of single-session therapy is that it provides therapy lasting one session only. They sometimes refer to this as 'one-off' therapy. These people then argue that in SST, we restrict help offered to people and only offer them one session when they want more. This is decidedly not the case.

However, the difficulty here is that single-session therapy *can* last for one session only. This occurs when the client states in advance that this is all they want, and the therapist concurs with this. Yet, single-session therapy can *also* refer to the situation mentioned above, where it can be one session but involves additional help. Young (2018) acknowledges the difficulties inherent in the term 'single-session therapy but argues for its retention because it has 'shock' value – it interests and challenges therapists new to this mode of therapy delivery. I understand this viewpoint, but as 'clarity' is one of the central principles in this area of discourse, I think that we should have a description of this way of working with people that is clear and accurate. Given the ambiguity surrounding the term 'single-session therapy', my approach is to look for a different, unambiguous descriptive term.

One-At-A-Time Therapy

Michael Hoyt (2011) introduced the term 'one at a time' to refer to SST. Hoyt, Bobele, Slive, Young and Talmon (2018: 5) state that this term describes the situation where 'therapy takes place one contact at a time, and one contact may be all the time that is needed'. However, particularly in counselling services in the United Kingdom, 'One-At-A-Time Therapy' (OAATT) has been used to describe a situation where students can only book one session at a time and in some services, what has been referred to as a 'purposeful pause'[4] has been imposed so that students have

---

[4] More formally here, at the end of the session, clients are asked to engage in a process called 'reflect-digest-act-let time pass-decide' where they are encouraged to reflect on their learning from the session, to digest it (meaning to make connections with other relevant areas of their life) to act on their reflections and digested learning and to see what happens before they decide to whether or not to seek more help. I have no objection to this when it is proposed as *one* way

to wait for a period, often two weeks before they can make another appointment. This practice reflects the situation in other agencies where clients are told that they will be contacted two weeks (for example) after their single session and asked how they are getting on and to see if they require further help. Therefore, one-at-a-time therapy excludes the possibility of the client deciding to make another appointment to see a therapist at the end of their single session. While this makes sense from an organisational perspective, it appears to be at variance with a central principle of this way of working with clients where the client is the principal decision-maker.

ONEplus Therapy

Given that I have reservations concerning the terms 'single-session therapy' and 'one-at-a-time therapy', what do I suggest instead? I have decided to call the mode of therapy delivery that is the subject of this book 'ONEplus therapy'. I have capitalised the word 'ONE' because it indicates it is a principal objective of this way of working to help the person with what they have come for by the end of the session. The word 'plus' is attached to the word 'ONE' without a space to indicate that more help is available to the client on request and that this is an integral part of the delivery mode. Unlike 'One-at-a-time therapy', 'ONEplus therapy' does not restrict *when* the person can access further help should they decide to do so. Also, the person can access any form of therapy delivery offered by the agency or practitioner. If they request a form of help not provided by the above, then, if possible, a suitable external referral is made.

In addition, given the dual nature of this way of working ('let's help you in one session/more help is available'), the term 'ONEplus therapy' does not suggest that only one session is offered to the client, which, in the minds of many, is suggested by the term 'single-session therapy'. Thus, I will use the term

---

forward after the session. My objection is when it is the *only* way forward for clients after the session.

'ONEplus therapy' in the rest of the book, which I define as follows:

> **ONEplus therapy is an intentional form of therapy delivery where the therapist and client contract to meet for a session of therapy and work together to help the client to achieve their stated wants from that session on the understanding that further help is available to the client on request.**

In Part I of this book, I will discuss what you need to do to prepare yourself to become a ONEplus therapist.

Part I

Preparing Yourself to Practise ONEplus Therapy

PREAMBLE

In Part I of this book, I will consider what you must do to prepare yourself to practise ONEplus therapy. You might think your initial therapy training was sufficient preparation in this respect, but I would beg to differ. The training you received was based on what I call the conventional therapy mindset, while your practice of ONEplus therapy needs to be under-pinned by a mindset more suited to this work. This mindset, which I refer to in this book as the ONEplus therapy mindset, suggests a way of working with clients you may not be familiar with. Thus, you need to be trained in ONEplus therapy.

Your ONEplus therapy trainer needs to be trained and experienced in delivering this way of working with clients. They need to create a training environment where you and your trainee colleagues feel free to ask questions, and voice doubts, reservations and objections (DROs) to the material the trainer is presenting. Then the trainer should respond to these questions and DROs with respect and clarity, correcting any misconceptions trainees express. In addition, the trainer needs to invite trainees to abide by the confidentiality principle of 'what is said here, stays here'. This is particularly important when some trainees volunteer for a demonstration session with the trainer and when all trainees work together in peer counselling (see Chapter 3).

Let me preview what is covered in ONEplus therapy training before discussing each element in greater detail.

- **Knowledge.** Learning about the nature of ONEplus therapy, its assumptions, the mindset that underpins its practice, and how this mindset informs practice.

- **Skills.** Learning and practising critical ONEplus therapy skills with members of your training group.

- **Supervised Practice.** Having your ONEplus therapy work with clients supervised by someone skilled in its practice.

2

Gaining Knowledge

To practise ONEplus therapy well, it is vital that you understand it fully. Thus, you need to be knowledgeable about ONEplus therapy in four main areas: its nature, the assumptions that underpin it, the mindset you need to have to practice it and the practice that stems from this mindset. I will deal with each area in turn.

The Nature of ONEplus Therapy

I defined ONEplus therapy at the end of Chapter 1 as 'an intentional form of therapy delivery where the therapist and client contract to meet for a session of therapy and work together to help the client to achieve their stated wants from that session on the understanding that further help is available to the client on request'. This definition shows the following important points:

ONEplus Therapy Has a Therapeutic Intention

Some therapy agencies are interested in offering ONEplus therapy to bring down waiting lists and reduce the time clients have to wait for a therapy appointment. While this is understandable from the agency's perspective, this is not ideally why ONEplus therapy should be offered to clients. The intention of ONEplus therapy is *therapeutic* rather than administrative. It is based on the idea that clients wish to be helped quickly and that many leave the session satisfied that they have got what they have come for and need no further help. Now, the introduction of ONEplus therapy into a therapy agency often has the

19

consequence of bringing down waiting lists and reducing waiting time, but this is different from saying that this is the *intention* of offering ONEplus therapy to clients.

ONEplus Therapy Is Contractual

It is a fundamental ethical principle of all forms of therapy that the client should give their informed consent about becoming a client before therapy is initiated. This is undoubtedly the case in ONEplus therapy. Seabury, Seabury and Garvin (2011) distinguish between an applicant and a client. An applicant is someone who applies for help from a therapist or a therapy agency and becomes a client once they have given their informed consent to proceed. You will need to provide your client with accurate information about ONEplus therapy and ensure that they understand it before proceeding with the session once they have provided their informed consent.[5] No client should have ONEplus therapy when they don't want it. Conversely, no therapist should be compelled to practise ONEplus therapy when they don't want to. The therapist's informed consent to practise ONEplus therapy also applies here.

ONEplus Therapy Privileges the Client's Wishes and Decisions

While most therapists will say that they are 'client-centred', they also proceed according to principles they hold dear but which may not be shared by their clients. Thus, they conduct an assessment or case history in the first session, assuming the client will return for another session. You, as a ONEplus therapist, do not make this latter assumption. Instead, you will ask your client what they want to achieve by the end of the session and proceed accordingly. You also go along with their decision concerning whether to seek additional help at the end of the session. I believe

---

[5] I will discuss this issue in Chapter 5.

that ONEplus therapy is a pluralistic form of therapy delivery because it privileges the client's wishes and decisions in the ways I have outlined (Cooper & McLeod, 2011). Does this mean you will stay silent if you have concerns about their wishes and decisions? Not at all. You will share your concerns and facilitate a discussion, but ultimately you recognise that the client will have the final say.

ONEplus Therapy is Collaborative

I mentioned above that although ONEplus therapy is client led, you are free to offer your viewpoint on the client's wishes and decision if you have any concerns. In these cases, I recommend you ask a question such as 'Are you interested in my perspective on what you want from the session?' What follows is an exchange of viewpoints, the goal of which is to discover a jointly agreed way forward. In this way, ONEplus therapy is collaborative. You work with the client to decide on the session's goal, focus, and ways in which the client can solve their problem if this is what they have come for. As a therapist, you must ensure that you do not impose your view on the client. Thus, it is part of your mindset as a ONEplus therapist (see below) to remember the previous point that the client predominantly leads ONEplus therapy.

In ONEplus Therapy, Further Help Is Available to the Client on Request

The final point is the one that prompted me to change the name of what I do from single-session therapy to ONEplus therapy. I mentioned in the previous chapter that the problem with the term 'single-session therapy' is that no matter how often the point is made to the contrary, people still think that it means that only one session will be provided to the client. This is not the case, but people can be forgiven for thinking that it is for the words in the phrase 'single-session therapy' can understandably be taken to mean a therapy that lasts for a single session. The term 'ONEplus therapy' does not have this meaning. The word 'plus' indicates that more help is available if the client requests it.

The Assumptions Underpinning ONEplus Therapy

All therapy delivery modes are based on certain assumptions, which is undoubtedly true for ONEplus therapy. In this section, I will present and discuss these assumptions.

A Brief Encounter Can Be Helpful

Most of us have experienced a brief encounter with someone who has been helpful to us. It is useful to stop for a moment and think of one meeting that somehow enriched your life. As you do so, ask yourself what it was about this interaction that was helpful to you. In addition, most of us have had the experience of helping someone briefly. We know we have had this experience because the person told us so later. What did they tell you about your brief encounter that was helpful to them? These experiences tell you that a person can be helped by another briefly, which is the case both inside and outside therapy.

Let me give a personal example of being helped by someone briefly. In my teenage years, I had a bad stammer. This led me to be anxious about speaking in public. One day, I was listening to a radio programme where Michael Bentine, a well-known comedian at that time, was interviewed. During this interview, Bentine mentioned that he also had a bad stammer when he was younger but learned to speak up despite this because he developed the following attitude towards stammering: 'If I stammer, I stammer – too bad!' This struck a chord with me then, and I resolved to develop this attitude by rehearsing it while speaking up without avoiding problematic words. This approach was helpful to me, and after a while, I could speak in public without anxiety, and although I still stammered, my stutter was far less pronounced than before. The relevant segment of the radio interview only lasted for a few minutes. Still, in that short period, I strongly resonated with the anti-anxiety attitude spelt out by Michael Bentine, and my subsequent use of that attitude resulted in long-term benefits.

Two exercises

I suggest that you engage in the following two exercises so that you can see what I mean by the idea that a brief encounter can be helpful:

Exercise 1: Being helped briefly
- Think of an episode where you were helped through a brief encounter with another person. This might have been someone you knew previously, or it might have been someone who was a stranger to you.
- Who was the person, and what did they do that was helpful to you?
- What did you take away from this encounter that was most helpful?
- What are the implications of your experience for ONEplus therapy?

Exercise 2: Helping someone else briefly
- Reflect on an occasion where you may have helped someone through having a brief encounter with them.
- What did you do that was helpful to the person?
- If you know, what did they take away that was most helpful to them?
- What are the implications of this episode for ONEplus therapy?

ONEplus therapy is a brief encounter, and it is assumed, therefore, that as such, it may be helpful to the client. Of course, it is also recognised that the person may not experience any benefit from the session.[6] In this case, they may request further help if they think doing so may benefit them.

A Person Can Help Themself Quickly

While you may help a client resolve a problem fully in a single session, it is more likely that such resolution will occur after the session when they have regularly implemented a solution that you helped them develop in the session. This is mainly the case when the person's problem is habitual. However, ONEplus therapy assumes people can help themselves quickly under certain conditions.

As an example, take the case of 'Vera'. She consulted Albert Ellis about an elevator phobia and joined one of his groups to tackle this issue. However, after several months she had yet to make progress. Then, one Friday, Vera consulted Ellis individually and told him she had to resolve her problem by Monday morning. Ellis asked her why, and she responded that up to now, she could walk up and down five floors of stairs to and from her office without using the elevator. However, her company had decided to move their office to the 105th floor of the same building, which would happen this weekend. 'Dr Ellis,' Vera exclaimed, 'you have to help me get over my problem quickly. I love and need my job, but there is no way I can walk up and down 105 floors.'

Ellis responded that she knew what to do. Repeatedly go up and down elevators until she had resolved the problem. She decided to do this, and by Sunday evening, she had lost her fear of elevators. Why did Vera not effect change before she knew about the office move but did so afterwards? My explanation is as follows.

---

[6] Hopefully, the client will not be harmed by the session, although this cannot be ruled out.

Knowing what to do to effect change

In both scenarios, Vera knew what to do to effect change. Such knowledge is often necessary, but more is needed to effect such change, particularly in habit-based problems.

Having a committed reason to change

In the first scenario, Vera did not have a committed reason to change. As she admitted, she could get by without tackling her problem. She could walk up and down five floors of stairs to and from her office without using the elevator. In the second scenario, she had to take action to keep her valued job. This was her committed reason to change.

Taking appropriate action

In the first scenario, Vera took no action to address her problem; in the second scenario, she did.

Being prepared to accept the costs of change, if any

Taking appropriate action in this context often involves a cost for the person. In Vera's case, this cost was the significant discomfort that a person experiences as they repeatedly expose themself to the phobic object, in this case, elevators. She was prepared to accept this cost because it was worth it to her to do so.

Time Is a Vital Motivating Factor

Consider someone who routinely procrastinates. The person is given a task and a time frame to do it. They put off doing the job until the very last minute when they gear themself into action and do a great deal of work quickly. This shows our relationship with time. When we have a lot of it, we make poor use of it; when we have little, we make the most of it. When applied to ONEplus therapy, the implications are clear. When the client and therapist have much time, they will use it but will progress slowly. When they have a small amount of time, they will use it efficiently, and the client will progress accordingly. This shows the role of time in ONEplus therapy and its role as a motivator for change.

The critical role time plays in ONEplus therapy is shown in two other areas. First, when a person quickly accesses ONEplus therapy at a time of their choosing, then they tend to get more out of the session than if they are put on a lengthy waiting list for it (see the section below on 'Help at the Point of Need'). Second, when time is used well between the making of a ONEplus therapy appointment and the session taking place (e.g., by the client preparing for the session), then again, the client will get more from the session than they will if they do nothing in the intervening period (see Chapter 7).

The Power of Now

One of the basic assumptions of ONEplus therapy is enshrined in the statement, 'the power of now'. This means that when you are with your client in ONEplus therapy, all you know is that you are with one another in the therapeutic space at that moment. You do not know if the person is likely to return, even if they say that they will. This means that the two of you need to decide what use you will make of the time you spend together. Here are your options:

1. Will you both engage in a therapy session focused on your client's stated wants?
2. Will you assess the client in preparation for later therapy?
3. Will you take the client's history to understand the person and their problems in their historical context?
4. Will you make a case formulation of the client's problems so that you know how they all fit together in the knowledge that doing so will help you both address these problems in the most appropriate order?

While all of these are valid ways of beginning a therapy session, when you work on the 'power of now' assumption, you will choose option 1.

All You Both Need Is Here

I see ONEplus therapy as a blend of what your client brings to the session (their issues, strengths, views and preferences) and what you bring (e.g., your expert knowledge and therapeutic skills). From this blend, the two of you can work together to help the client get unstuck from their nominated issue and begin to take healthy steps forward. All you need to do this is present in the therapeutic space where you are meeting.

Help at the Point of Need

The final assumption of ONEplus therapy that I want to present is that a person should be helped at the point of their need rather than at the point where the agency to which they have applied for help can provide them with an appointment. In the latter scenario, the usual practice is for a client to be given an initial appointment where they are assessed by a representative of that agency to determine what help the agency thinks the person needs. There is usually a wait for such an assessment appointment. Then after the person has been assigned to a particular form of help determined by the agency, there is another wait for a therapy appointment to be offered. At that first therapy appointment, the treating therapist will likely assess the patient in a more detailed manner than at the previous assessment session, take a case history, and/or conduct a case formulation. Then therapy will begin.[7] Contrast this with ONEplus therapy, either by appointment or

---

[7] The American Psychiatric Association defines psychotherapy, or talk therapy as 'a way to help people with a broad variety of mental illnesses and emotional difficulties. It can help eliminate or control troubling symptoms so a person can function better and can increase well-being and healing.' https://www.psychiatry.org/patients-families/psychotherapy

open access walk-in, where therapy commences the moment the client first meets the therapist. This will be as soon as the person accesses a walk-in ONEplus therapy clinic or within a week of making an appointment at a ONEplus therapy by-appointment agency.

The ONEplus Therapy Mindset and How It Informs Practice

What is the most crucial ingredient in helping you to become a skilled ONEplus therapist? My answer to this question is the mindset you bring to ONEplus therapy. Cannistrà (2022: 1) states that a mindset is 'the therapist's series of beliefs which influence the actions and decisions taken in the course of their work'. In this section, I will outline the main elements of the ONEplus therapy mindset, which you are advised to bring to your implementation of this mode of therapy delivery. I will also show how this mindset informs the practice of ONEplus Therapy. Compare this mindset with what I call the 'conventional therapy mindset' that underpins the delivery of traditional therapy, where the client and therapist are expected to spend more than one session together, often a lot more (see Appendix 1).

One Session or More: Be Open to Both Possibilities

As I have emphasised, the defining feature of ONEplus therapy is that you and the client meet to help the person take away from the session what they have come for on the understanding that more help is available to the person on request. It would be best to keep both ideas in mind as you approach the session and be open to both possibilities, prioritising neither. This principle informs the practice of ONEplus therapy, particularly at the end of the session when you will review the client's options for additional help.

It Is Possible to Conduct a Session Without Prior Knowledge of the Person

As I will discuss in the following chapter, some ONEplus therapists send their clients a pre-session form to complete, primarily to help their clients prepare for their session to get the most from it. These clients are invited to share their completed forms with their therapists so that the latter can also prepare for the session. Clients are informed that the completion and/or return of the form is not mandatory, just recommended. Some clients choose not to complete the form; others do it but decide not to return it. This does not mean that they can't have the session. In your case, it means seeing the client with no prior information. This is acceptable in ONEplus therapy, where seeing clients without prior knowledge about them is common. For example, this frequently happens in open access, walk-in therapy, and all the time when I do live demonstrations of ONEplus therapy for professionals (Dryden, 2021).

Indeed, sometimes having prior knowledge about a client can pose a problem. Thus, a client may return their pre-session preparation form stating that they want to address an anger issue, but on the day, they want to discuss an anxiety problem. If you expect to deal with the former, you may need to prepare to deal with the latter. It may throw you. So, it is vital to keep in mind any information you may have about a client and be prepared to let it go in favour of the client's stated wants from the session.

While some therapists who offer more ongoing forms of therapy require a referral letter or insist upon an assessment session before deciding on whether to offer therapy to a client, not having knowledge about a client is no barrier to seeing someone in ONEplus therapy.

Start Therapy from the First Moment

It is vital to remember that the purpose of the first (and perhaps only) ONEplus therapy session you will have with the client is to provide them with the form of help they seek, not the form of help you think they need. This is reflected in how you begin the session, which I will discuss in Chapter 8. Volunteers at the Samaritans[8] answer calls to their telephone line with 'Hello, the Samaritans. How can I help you?' and not with 'Hello, the Samaritans, How can I assess you?' Thus, as a ONEplus therapist, remember that you are there to provide straightaway the therapeutic help requested by the client unless there is a good reason not to do so. Consequently, you will cut to the therapeutic chase at the outset and ask one of several questions designed to initiate therapy immediately (see Chapter 8).

View the Session as a Whole, Complete in Itself

As a ONEplus therapist, you approach the session as if it is the only time that you will meet the person (while allowing for the possibility that it might not be) and that this will be a complete session that lasts for a duration determined by both of you.[9] This being said, there *may* be pre-session contact through the completion and return of a form, and there *may* be post-session contact when the client requests further help. Also, the session has its process with a beginning, a middle and an end.

Potentially Anyone Can Be Helped in a Single Session

One of the questions people frequently ask me during the training workshops I offer in ONEplus therapy is which clients can and cannot be helped in a single session of ONEplus therapy. It would

---

[8] The Samaritans is a registered charity aimed at providing emotional support to anyone in emotional distress, struggling to cope or at risk of suicide throughout the United Kingdom and the Republic of Ireland, often through its telephone helpline.

[9] Sessions in ONEplus therapy can be of varying lengths. In my practice, I offer a client a session of up to 50 minutes. I do this because if we finish earlier, then it's better to end the session when the work is done than when the clock determines session's end. I also work for an online service which offers clients 30-minute video therapy sessions. While clients can have from 5 to 8 sessions, most attend one session.

be best if you learned as a ONEplus therapist that you could help *anyone*, but you will not be able to help *everyone*. Given that you will only be able to know if your client found the session helpful at the end of the session, you should not decline to help someone until it becomes clear that you can't. This is a significant principle behind open access, walk-in therapy and is one of the ways in which this mode of therapy delivery influences ONEplus therapy by appointment. Consequently, you do not need to engage in any pre-therapy exploration with the client concerning their suitability or non-suitability for ONEplus therapy. The critical issue is whether your client understands ONEplus therapy and wants to access it. If the answer to the first question is 'no', help them to understand it. Then, if the answer to the second question is 'no', don't proceed with ONEplus therapy but discover what help they wish to access and offer it to them if you or the agency in which you work can do so.

Focus on the Person, Not the Disorder

Following on from the above, it is vital that you bring to ONEplus therapy the focus on your client as a unique individual and not as a representative of a category indicating a mental health disorder. Thus, when I am asked a question such as, 'Can you help someone with "x" disorder in ONEplus therapy?' my response is, 'What is the person's name, and what do they want to achieve from the session?'

This focus on the person and not the disorder is demonstrated in the following example. A person diagnosed with psychosis sought help from a walk-in clinic in a state of anxiety. What had been happening was that the client's landlord had found him agitated, talking to himself and was concerned that the client posed a risk to others in his building. He, thus, threatened the client with eviction. In the session, the therapist first responded by suggesting that the client might wish to review his medication with his psychiatrist, which he agreed to do. Then, as the client stated that his goal was to keep his accommodation, the therapist suggested that they role-played how the client could talk to his landlord to allay the latter's fears about the client posing a risk to the household. They did this, and the client implemented this solution with his landlord and successfully retained his accommodation. He was still diagnosed as psychotic, but he was psychotic and safe in his living quarters rather than psychotic and vulnerable living on the streets.

Again, the answer to the question, can this person with a disorder benefit from ONEplus therapy, is that if they understand it and want to access it, offer it to them and see if they benefit from it by the end of the session.

The Client–Therapist Relationship Can Be Established Rapidly

Another frequently asked question about ONEplus therapy concerns the questioner's doubts about whether a productive relationship can be established with the client in this mode of service delivery. My response is a resounding, 'Yes, it can.' Taking Bordin's (1979) tripartite view of the working alliance and my elaboration of it (Dryden, 2011), the following explains why I am clear in my answer. A good working alliance between client and therapist is demonstrated by the pair having a good bond, shared views about therapy, an agreement on the client's goals and an agreed pathway towards these goals.

In ONEplus therapy, a good working alliance is evidenced by the following:

Shared views

You and your client agree to meet to help the client take away from the session their stated wants (the 'ONE' in ONEplus therapy) and on the understanding that more help is available to the client on request (the 'plus' in ONEplus therapy).

Agreement on the client's goal

You and your client agree that the focus will be on what the client wants to achieve from the session.

Effective bond

You show respect for the client (a) by demonstrating a keenness to help the person in the way that they wish to be helped, (b) by expressing your understanding of how the client sees things, and (c) by being transparent about what you can do and can't do.

Agreed pathway towards the client's goals (agreed tasks)

Once you have established the client's preferred way of being helped, you adjust your intervention to match the client's preferences in this respect. Most of the time, this will be the client wanting a solution to their problem. In this case, your task is to help them discover a solution they can integrate into their life and implement after the session.

Simon, Imel, Ludman and Steinfeld (2012) found that those clients who benefited from a single session of therapy reported forming a better working alliance with their therapists along the above lines than clients who did not benefit from it.

Be Transparent

It is very important that you are transparent as a ONEplus therapist.[10] This means that you are clear about the following:

- What ONEplus therapy is and what it isn't.
- What you can do and can't do in ONEplus therapy.
- What further help is available, and how long your client has to wait for it.
- The reasons for your interventions.
- Answering any questions your client has about ONEplus therapy.

---

[10] One way in which you can facilitate this is by sending potential ONEplus therapy clients an explanatory leaflet about ONEplus therapy (see Appendix 2).

ONEplus Therapy Is Client Led

One of the most critical aspects of the ONEplus therapy mindset is that the client determines what happens in ONEplus therapy. This is demonstrated by the client taking the lead:

- By indicating the help that they are seeking from the therapist.
- By setting the goal for the session.
- By playing an active role in creating a focus for the session.
- By selecting what they regard as the best solution to their nominated problem.

As a ONEplus therapist, you will keep these points in mind in working with the client in this form of therapy delivery and make interventions to encourage them to take the lead.

The Client Decides How Much Therapy They Want

In many therapy agencies, the agency decides how much therapy a client will get. In such cases, the client is offered a block of sessions – often six – which may be reviewed again, mainly at the behest of the therapist. In ONEplus therapy, the client decides how much therapy they want, often opting for a single session because they have received the help they had been looking for from that session. Unless you have internalised this mindset principle, you will tend to think during the session that the client needs more therapy because you can discern beneath the surface of the client's narrative that they have more problems that require therapeutic attention. When reviewing the client's future options concerning further help, if *you* think they need more help, you will express this opinion in some way that may influence the client to select the additional help option at the end of the session.

When you adopt the principle that the client decides how much therapy they want at the end of the session, you will say something like:

'We have three ways forward, and each option is equally fine. Thus, you can decide that you have gotten the help you have come for and don't need further help. You can decide that you need further help, and we can discuss what kind of help that might be and book an appointment now. Finally, you can decide that you would like some time to implement your takeaways from the session, see how things go and contact us later if you would like more help. As I have said, each option is equally OK. Which option is the best one for you?'

Identify and Meet the Client's Preference for Being Helped

While the most frequently requested form of help that clients seek from ONEplus therapy is with a specific emotional or behavioural problem with which they feel stuck, this is by no means the only type of help you can offer as a ONEplus therapist. When you ask your client what kind of help they are looking for from you, they may be unable to respond with clarity. Thus, they may need clarification about what type of help they seek, in which case you can outline the various helping options on offer. Therefore, you can help them to:

- Develop a greater understanding of their nominated issue.
- Talk about the issue while you listen.
- Express their feelings about the issue.
- Solve an emotional or behavioural problem with which they feel stuck.
- Make a decision.
- Resolve a dilemma.
- Talk about whatever they want to talk about in their own way.

In addition, they may wish you to:

- Give them your professional opinion on something or
- Signpost them to appropriate services.

Having outlined these helping options, you can then ask them to select the one that most closely matches the help they seek. Such matching is important. As Norcross and Cooper (2021) note, when the therapist helps the client in the way they wish to be helped, rather than in the way the therapist thinks the client needs, then a better therapeutic outcome is more likely.

Keep in Mind the Importance of Negotiating an End-of-Session Goal with the Client

When the client is asked about their goals in conventional therapy, it is what they want to achieve by the end of therapy. In ONEplus therapy, you ask your client what they want to accomplish by the end of the session. This emphasis on a session goal helps to focus your both and provides a direction for the session.

I distinguish between a session goal and a problem-related goal. The latter is what the client wants to achieve in relation to their nominated problem. In this context, a session goal can be finding a solution to the nominated problem that the client can implement to work towards achieving their problem-related goal. This is shown diagrammatically thus:

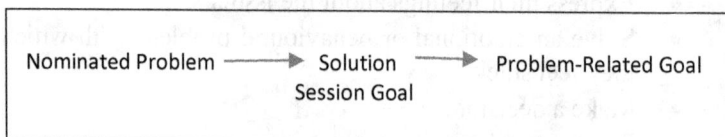

Nominated Problem ⟶ Solution ⟶ Problem-Related Goal
Session Goal

Keep in Mind the Importance of Co-creating a Therapeutic Focus and Maintaining It Once It Has Been Created

Aside from the situation where the client wants to have the opportunity to talk about whatever they want to talk about in whichever way they want to talk about it, ONEplus therapy is best done with focus. This focus needs to be co-created with the client and should be related to the session goal and address the client's nominated problem, if relevant.

Once the focus has been decided upon, it is important to maintain it. It is your responsibility as a ONEplus therapist to do this. You may need to interrupt the client to help them to return to the focus if they have moved away from it. The best way to do this is to give a rationale for interrupting the client, gain their assent for you to do this, and agree on how you will interrupt them. It is also helpful to check in periodically with your client to determine that they are still discussing what they want to talk about with you.

Unless the Client's Preference Is to the Contrary, a ONEplus Therapy Session Requires a Structure

As I pointed out earlier, you can provide different types of help in ONEplus therapy. That being said, the most common form of help clients seek from this mode of therapy delivery is emotional/behavioural problem-solving. Providing such help means adhering to a particular structure for the session. This is as follows:

The beginning phase

Here, you and your client agree on the purpose of the session and make a contract for the session. Then you decide on a goal for the session with the client and co-create a focus. You then assess the client's nominated problem.[11]

---

[11] ONEplus therapists who practise solution focused therapy may omit this step.

The middle phase

In the middle phase of ONEplus therapy, the emphasis is on helping the client to find a solution to their nominated problem. Here, several relevant factors come into play, including previous helpful attempts to address the problem, the opposite of the factors that maintain the client's problem, the client's internal strengths and external resources, the client's view of what may help and your view of what may help. Different solutions may be discussed until one is settled on, and at this point, you can help the client to rehearse the solution, if feasible. You can then help the client to think of ways to implement this solution, and finally, you may wish to work with the client to identify and address obstacles to such implementation.

The end phase

At this point, you are ready to bring the session to a close. First, you can ask the client to summarise what you have covered in the session. In particular, you will wish to encourage the client to identify their takeaways from the session and review how they will implement these in their life. If possible, encourage them to see how they can generalise their learning to other problems that they may have. Before you finish, you will be minded to allow your client to ask any last-minute questions, which you will answer and to tell you anything that wraps things up for them. Stress that this is not an opportunity to discuss a new problem. End the session by reminding them that they can get more help if they wish.

Complex Problems Do Not Always Require Complex Solutions

The point is often made that ONEplus therapy is not suitable to help people with complex problems because they need far more time than a single session to be helped. My response is, 'It depends.' First, you may be able to help a person with a complex problem because although a problem may be complex, it does not follow that the solution has to be complex. Second, a person with a complex problem may seek help for another problem that is not complex. Third, the person with a complex problem may benefit from taking a 'one step at a time' approach to this problem. Finally, remember that ONEplus therapy does not preclude the person from having ongoing therapy for their complex problem should this option be available to them and they choose to use it.

Focus on What the Person Has Done Before Concerning the Problem

Usually, your client will have made several attempts to help themself with their problem. As they still have the problem, you might be excused for thinking that nothing that they have done in the past to help themself has any merit. However, this is not necessarily the case. It is worthwhile for you to consider the importance of reviewing with the client what they did in the past to address the issue and what was in any way helpful to them and what was not beneficial.

You can also think of doing this with how they have addressed similar and non-similar problems in the past. This may help you to identify strategies that the client has successfully used in the past that they may be able to transfer to the work you are doing together on their nominated problem.

One question that can be particularly helpful is, 'Think of a personal problem that you solved in the past that, as you look back, you are particularly proud of. What did you do that you were most proud of?' This question can be useful in two ways. First, it can give you and your client *specific* information about what they can use to address their nominated problem in ONEplus therapy. Second, it may give your client a *general* sense of their ability to be a good problem-solver that they may use to address their current issue.

Focus on the Client's Internal Strengths and External Resources

As a ONEplus therapist, you need to hold in mind that if you are to help the person take away what they have come for from the session, you will need to identify and make use of both the client's internal strengths and external resources that are available to them that they can use. When you do this, you encourage the client to address their problem under favourable conditions. Failing to do this is like trying to repair a building with shaky foundations. First, strengthen the foundations and then repair. Here are some ways of eliciting such information in the course of ONEplus therapy:

Internal strengths

In the course of the client telling you about their nominated problem and how they have tried to address it in the past, you will be able to hear the client express strengths that they have. In your responses, you can refer to these as strengths that the client may use in addressing the problem and discuss how they might do so. You can also ask your client for their strengths more directly (see Chapter 9).

External resources

Again, when the client tells you about their nominated problem and how they have tried to address it, they may refer to other people. Determine which people have been helpful to the client and how they have been of help. Encourage your client to consider recruiting these people as they work towards addressing their nominated problem after the session has finished. See Chapter 9 for specific questions you can ask here.

In making suggestions to your client about potentially useful organisations and other external resources, don't overwhelm them with too much information. One or two suggestions will suffice.

Keep in Mind that Different Methods Can Be Used with Different Clients

Given that ONEplus clients differ from one another, and they will want different things from the session, it is vital to bear this in mind when considering what help to offer them. When considering this, does it make sense for you to approach the session thinking that no matter what clients bring, you will use the same methods with each of them? Of course, not. So, remember that you will need to use different methods with different clients.

You can check with clients what type of methods they may find helpful. In this respect, I have found it useful to ask the client if they find imagery methods helpful. If so, I will make use of such methods during the session.

Be Solution-Focused, If Relevant

As I made clear above, as a ONEplus therapist, you need to be prepared to approach the session remembering that different clients will be seeking different forms of help from you, and you should be prepared to offer them the help that they seek unless there is a good reason not to do so. You should also note that most people seeking ONEplus therapy will do so because they seek help with a specific emotional/behavioural problem with which they have become stuck. When this is the case, remember that you need to help them find a solution to their nominated problem. Recall that a solution addresses the nominated problem and allows the person to achieve their problem-related goal. A solution can involve your client in the following:

- Developing a new way of thinking.
- Changing a relevant attitude.
- Developing a new constructive way of acting (e.g. being assertive).
- Altering some aspect(s) of the environment.

- Developing a new habit to promote their mental well-being (e.g. practising mindfulness regularly).
- Developing a new habit to promote their physical well-being (e.g. taking regular exercise).

In addition, a solution may involve some combination of the above factors.

When developing a solution with the person, it is vital that you and your client draw from the following:

- Helpful aspects of your client's previous attempts to solve the problem.
- Helpful aspects of your client's attempts to solve other problems, related and unrelated to the nominated problem.
- Constructive alternatives to problem-maintaining factors.
- Your client's relevant strengths.
- Relevant aspects of the external resources available to your client.
- The solution that your client's relevant role model would use.
- Your client's views on what would constitute a good solution.
- Your views on what would constitute a good solution.

Please remember that you and your client should select from the above list and only attempt to include some, not all, factors. It is also vital that you both consider that your client is most likely to use a solution regularly that they can integrate into their life. For example, if practising mindfulness is deemed a good solution, you should consider where and when your client can best carry out this practice.

Promote In-session Practice, If Feasible

In the same way, you would probably not drive a car without taking it out for a test drive, your client needs to rehearse (or 'test drive) a solution before committing to it. This rehearsal aims for your client to understand what it feels like to use the solution and to judge its effectiveness.

When suggesting in-session rehearsal of solutions, you can draw on the following:

- Imagery methods
- Role-play
- Two-chair dialogue
- Parts work methods

The outcome of this rehearsal may be that your client:

- Accepts the solution
- Makes changes to the solution
- Rejects the solution

In the latter case, your client would seek a different solution, and the client would rehearse this as above. This process would continue until the client has accepted a solution.

Help the Client Plan for Action

A solution is only helpful if implemented, and this is an essential point for you to keep in mind while conducting a ONEplus therapy session. Also, keep in mind the factors that will encourage your client to implement their action plan:

- They can integrate the plan into their life.
- They are clear on when to implement the plan, where to implement it and how frequently.
- They keep in mind the reason for implementing the plan.

- They can identify and deal with any obstacles to them implementing the plan.

Small May Be Beautiful

A phenomenon known as quantum change is a sudden, dramatic, and enduring change that affects a broad range of emotions, cognitions and behaviour (Miller & C' de Baca, 2001). While this can happen in ONEplus therapy, it rarely does. What is more common in this service delivery is that the client makes a small but significant step away from their problem towards their problem-related goal or begins to free themself from a stuck pattern. In the same way that a gardener learns to identify and nurture the early shoots of a recently planted seed, both you and your client should learn to see that such small steps towards growth in the client are, indeed, beautiful and should be encouraged.

Have the Client Summarise the Session

As you approach the end of the ONEplus therapy session, think about how your client can consolidate what they have learned from the session. One way of doing this is to ask them to summarise the session. This helps them stay active in the session and allows them to think about what has stood out for *them* from the session. If you summarise the session for the client, you show them what has stood out for *you* and render them passive at the very point that they need to be active. By all means, add to the client's summary, but let it still be their summary.

Focus on the Client's Takeaway(s)

What your client learns from the session is important, but if they do not take their learning away, they haven't gotten the most from the session. Asking what the client will take away from the session and their plans to implement it is a vital part of the process. In doing this, remind them of the work you may have already done with them on action planning. If you have not done this work, now is the time to do it. In ONEplus therapy, less is more, so it is vital that you do not press your client to take away more than one or two significant learning points that, if implemented, would make a meaningful difference to their life.

Encourage Generalisation Whenever Possible

When the client has nominated a problem for which they are seeking help, your prime responsibility in ONEplus therapy is to help them develop a solution to this problem so that they can practice and achieve their problem-related goal. Once you have done that and if you have time, it is useful if you consider the idea that it is helpful to ask the client to determine how they may generalise this solution to other relevant situations and problem areas. It is vital that you think about how to build this into the fabric of the session since most clients will not generalise their learning as a matter of course.

Results are Mainly Achieved Outside the Session

As discussed above, while what happens in the session between you and your client is important in laying the foundations for change, what happens outside the session subsequently is more critical in determining what the client achieves from ONEplus therapy. It is important that you bear this in mind as you work with your client.

End the Session Well So That the Client Leaves the Session with Their Morale Restored

In viewing the session as a whole (see above), remember that it is vital to end the session well so that the client can leave with a sense of hope, having had their morale restored. You want the client to leave with all their questions answered and have the opportunity to tell you everything they wanted. You will also need to be clear about their options for accessing further help.

Take Nothing for Granted

Finally, the ONEplus therapist treats their inferences about what the client is capable of and the potency of the external resources available to them as hypotheses to be confirmed or disconfirmed. Holding to this principle means that the therapist takes nothing for granted and will respond to what happens in the session as it unfolds.

See Table 1 for a review of the elements of the ONEplus therapy mindset and commonly expressed doubts, reservations and objections (DROs) that therapists not steeped in ONEplus therapy make concerning this mode of therapy delivery.

Having outlined what you need to know about ONEplus therapy, I will discuss general core skills that underpin the good practice of this form of therapy delivery in the next chapter.

Table 1 Elements of the ONEplus therapy mindset, and common doubts, reservations and objections (DROs) that therapists not steeped in this mindset make about each element

Elements of the ONEplus Therapy Mindset	Doubts, Reservations and Objections
• One session or more. Be open to both possibilities	• There is little that can be done in one session, so it's important to offer more
• It is possible to conduct a session without prior knowledge of the person	• It is essential to have information about a client before seeing them
• Start therapy from the first moment	• Start therapy with carrying out an assessment and taking a case history
• View the session as a whole, complete in itself	• The first session is the first of many
• Potentially anyone can be helped in a single session	• Very few clients can be helped in one session of therapy
• Focus on the person, not the disorder	• It's important to discover what disorder the person is suffering from in order to know how to treat them
• The client-therapist relationship can be established rapidly	• The client-therapist relationship takes quite a while to establish
• Be transparent	• Being transparent may interfere with the development of the transference

Table 1 (continued)

Elements of the ONEplus Therapy Mindset	Doubts, Reservations and Objections
• ONEplus therapy is client led	• Therapy is therapist led
• The client decides how much therapy they want	• The therapist decides how much therapy the client needs
• Identify and meet the client's preference for being helped	• The help the client may prefer may not be the help they need
• Keep in mind the importance of negotiating an end-of-session goal with the client	• The goal of the first session should be to make sure that the client comes back for the second
• Keep in mind the importance of co-creating a therapeutic focus and maintaining it once it has been created	• Based on a thorough assessment and case formulation, the therapist suggests the focus of therapy
• Unless the client's preference is to the contrary, a ONEplus therapy session requires a structure	• At the beginning of therapy, there should be little structure to enable the client to discuss what they want in their own way
• Complex problems do not always require complex solutions	• Complex problems require complex treatments
• Focus on what the client has done before concerning the problem	• It's not necessary to know what the client has done before concerning the problem. The case formulation will show what the client needs to do now

Table 1 (continued)

Elements of the ONEplus Therapy Mindset	Doubts, Reservations and Objections
• Focus on the client's internal strengths and external resources	• Focus on the client's problems
• Keep in mind that different methods can be used with different clients	• Internal consistency in therapy is important
• Be solution focused, if relevant	• It is vital to be problem focused as their problems are what has brought the client to therapy
• Promote in-session practice, if feasible	• The in-session transference relationship needs to developed and interpreted
• Help the client plan for action	• Taking action occurs at the end of therapy
• Small may be beautiful	• A small change is insufficient to help with difficult issues
• Have the client summarise the session	• The therapist should summarise the work, not the client
• Focus on the client's takeaway(s)	• Focus on deepening the therapeutic relationship
• Encourage generalisation, whenever possible	• Generalisation will occur naturally when the client has worked through important issues

Table 1 (continued)

Elements of the ONEplus Therapy Mindset	Doubts, Reservations and Objections
• Results are mainly achieved outside the session	• Results are mainly achieved inside the session
• End the session well so that the client leaves the session with their morale restored	• Allow a session to end how it ends
• Take nothing for granted	• There are therapeutic factors that are reliably associated with change and gives therapy a sense of coherence

3

Developing General Skills

Knowing what to do is a vital part of training to become a ONEplus therapist. If you don't know what to do, you will be at a loss to help someone. However, knowing what to do is insufficient in ONEplus therapy practice. You need to be able to translate that knowledge into action. It is important to realise that a vital part of ONEplus therapy training involves developing your therapeutic skills in this mode of therapy delivery.

This is best done within the training context in peer counselling, where you and one of your trainee colleagues pair up, taking turns to be therapist and client. When you are a therapist, you help the other address a real and current problem for which they would like help from you. You do this in front of a group of your colleagues and your trainer. The latter will take the lead in offering you feedback on your skills as a ONEplus therapist. Ideally, you will have several such opportunities to receive feedback on your skills while on your training course.

While your trainer will take the lead in offering you feedback, you will also receive feedback from the rest of the observing group and, most importantly, from the person who was your client. The latter's feedback will tell you what it felt like being helped by you from the client's perspective.

Appendix 3 provides an evaluation sheet that I have used when assessing the skills demonstrated by trainees as therapists during their final assessed peer ONEplus counselling session.

What follows is a discussion of key *general* skills that ONEplus therapy trainees particularly struggle with during their training. In particular, I will discuss the following:

- The use of questions
- Being goal-directed
- Focusing
- Being clear in your communications and clarifying your client's communications

I will discuss more *specific* skills in Part III of this book.

The Use of Questions

When I initially trained in therapy, asking clients questions was almost forbidden. This was because doing so was invariably from our frame of reference as a therapist, whereas what we should be doing was to convey our understanding of our clients from their frame of reference. Other therapists are wary of asking clients questions because they think doing so gets in the way of clients discussing what they wish to discuss. So, one of the ONEplus therapist trainer's tasks is to provide a plausible rationale for using questions in ONEplus therapy. I usually explain that apart from the rare occasion when a client wishes to spend the session just talking freely and without interruption, ONEplus therapy requires a focus. One of the best ways of helping the client to select and keep to a focus is by asking questions. In addition, asking questions helps you as a ONEplus therapist to do the following:

- Assess the client's nominated problem.
- Help the client to identify their inner strengths and external resources.
- Discover the client's previous attempts to solve their problem.
- Help the client to select potential solutions to their problem.
- Invite the client to rehearse their chosen solution.
- Help the client to develop an action plan to implement their solution.

- Help the client to identify and address potential obstacles to action implementation.
- Invite the client to summarise the session.
- Invite the client to identify their takeaways.
- Invite the client to think about whether or not they want further help and, if so, what help they wish to access.

Difficulties with Using Questions in ONEplus Therapy

Trainees learning ONEplus therapy tend to have several difficulties using questions in the mode of therapy delivery. I will now list them and show how they can be rectified.

Asking multiple questions instead of one

You may do this when your client hasn't answered the question immediately or if you feel uncertain about the question yourself and want to clarify or correct it. The trouble with asking multiple questions when one will do is that your client becomes confused. So even if your client does not answer the question immediately or if you feel uncertain about your first question, hold off on asking another until your client indicates they don't understand the question. Then ask it again using a different form of words.

Not giving the client time to answer a question

There may be several reasons why a client does not answer a question immediately. However, it is a good rule of thumb to give the client time to think even if they may not use it for thinking. This means that you need to resist the temptation to fill the silence, Trainees who particularly 'feel' pressured by the fact that they may not see the client again tend to have this issue. For such trainees, I suggest going into a bare room and doing nothing for 50 minutes to experience how long this period is. They invariably say that it feels much longer than they thought. This exercise helps them calm down and allows them to give their clients more time to think than before.

Not responding appropriately when your client gives an immediate 'I don't know' in response to your questions

Some clients in ONEplus therapy will immediately reply, 'I don't know', to questions you may ask. There may be several reasons they may do this.

First, they generally do not know the answer to the question. However, the immediate nature of their response belies the possibility that they don't know the answer since they may have been able to answer it if they had given the matter some thought. In this case, you may say, 'You said, "I don't know" really quickly. Just take some time to think about the question before you answer it.'

Second, they prefer you to use your brain as a ONEplus therapist rather than their brain as a ONEplus therapy client. In response to your questions, saying, 'I don't know', invites you to do more work in the process. If you accept this invitation, you will, indeed, do more work than the client, who becomes passive in the process. Once you have identified this pattern, you can respond in a way that encourages client participation. For example:

Therapist: What do you think you were anxious about in that situation?

Client (immediately): I don't know.

Therapist: Give it a bit more thought before you respond.

Client (after a slightly longer gap): I don't know.

Therapist: What are the possibilities?

Third, the client may find a question challenging or uncomfortable and say, 'I don't know', to fend off the challenge or discomfort. One way you could respond here is to find out what the client was feeling, and if they were feeling uncomfortable, for example, you can explore and deal with the source of their discomfort. However, doing this may take you too far from the agreed focus of the session. In which case, you can proceed as follows:

Therapist:	How did you feel when I asked you that question?
Client:	Uncomfortable.
Therapist:	So, saying, 'I don't know', resulted in what?
Client:	It relieved me of discomfort.
Therapist:	OK, there are a few ways forward. We can stay away from this question because you find it uncomfortable. We can stick with the question even though you find it uncomfortable. Or you can tell me how I can ask you the question so you don't feel uncomfortable. Which would be the most productive for you?

Not responding when your client has not answered an important question

Many years ago, a friend doing a PhD at a famous Portuguese university fell out with his supervisor. The university asked me to take over as his supervisor, which I agreed to do. Before his viva, which in Portugal is a significant public event, the head of his department came over. He said that as people knew I was a friend of the candidate, I needed not to show favouritism to him during the viva. I agreed. During the viva, I asked my friend a series of warm-up questions, which he answered satisfactorily. Then I asked him an important question, to which he gave a lengthy response in which he did not answer my question. I responded thus: 'Mr Ronaldo,[12] you have given a lengthy response to a question which I did not ask you. Now, please answer the question I did ask you.' The gasps from the audience showed that I was not showing my friend any favouritism.

---

[12] Not the candidate's name.

By telling you this story, I am not advocating being blunt with a client in ONEplus therapy who does not answer an important question. Far from it. Instead, I urge you to pay particular attention to a client's response, mainly if you ask an important question. If so, you can say, 'I'm sorry, I don't think I have been clear in asking my question. Let me ask it differently.' If they continue to answer a different question, you might ask them to put your question into your own words and correct them if necessary. Alternatively, you might say, 'I sense that my question is not easy for you to answer directly. Is that so?' If that is the case, you need to find a constructive way forward with your client. This may involve the client answering the question their way, the two of you discussing why it is a difficult question for them, or you both choosing to leave the question unanswered.

The Appropriate Use of Open, Choice-Based and Closed Questions

In ONEplus therapy, there is no rule that stipulates which questions to ask and which to avoid asking. Consequently, you can ask open-ended, choice-based, and closed questions, but you need to do so appropriately. This, you can ask:

- Open-ended questions to encourage the client to speak more fully about an issue (e.g. 'Please tell me a little about what you feel angry about')

- Choice-based questions when you want the client to choose between alternatives (e.g., 'When you felt anxious about receiving feedback from your boss, did you hold the attitude, 'I want him to give me good feedback and therefore he must do so' or the attitude, 'I want him to give me good feedback, but he does not have to do so'?)

- Closed questions when you want a yes or no answer from the client (e.g., 'Did the person look threatening to you?')

Being Goal-Directed

ONEplus therapy is goal-directed, so you must skilfully encourage your client to set workable goals. Two sets of goals are particularly relevant in ONEplus therapy: session goals and problem-related goals.

Session Goals

As has been mentioned several times, as a ONEplus therapist, you do not know if you will see your client again, so, in light of this, you strive to help them achieve their stated wants from the session. These stated wants are frequently equivalent to the solutions they seek to help them with their problem. Often your client says they want to gain some tools and techniques to help them with their problem. My response is to ask them whether they think it is best to learn what tools and techniques are available once they have understood their problem better or without such understanding. The client almost always says it is best to understand their problem first and then derive suitable tools and techniques from such understanding. This is shown diagrammatically below:

Session goal: To discover tools and techniques to deal with the nominated problem

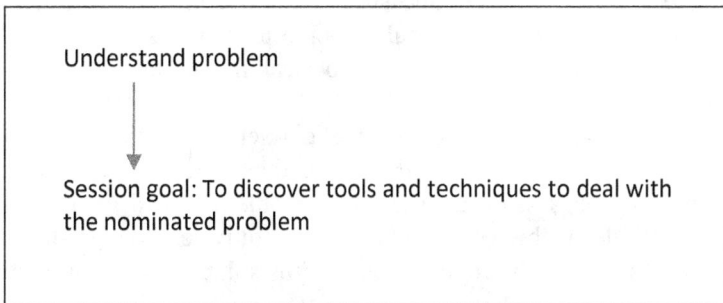

Understand problem

Session goal: To discover tools and techniques to deal with the nominated problem

Problem-Related Goals

In addition to specifying a session goal, your client may indicate a problem-related goal. This is what they want to achieve related to their problem. For example, if their nominated problem is anxiety about public speaking, their goal might be to be non-anxiously concerned about speaking in public. Such concern is realistic and far less likely to stop the client from speaking in public than anxiety. Instead, suppose the client states that their goal is not to feel anxious about public speaking. In that case, this goal is problematic because it involves the absence of a state ('I don't want to be anxious') rather than the presence of a state (un-anxious concern as above). Thus, whenever a client states the absence of a state as a problem-related goal, you need to address this and encourage them to state the presence of a realistic and healthy state instead.

Now suppose that the client suggests the presence of a positive state as a problem-related goal (e.g., 'I want to enjoy public speaking'). This is troublesome because it is unrealistic for a client to go from being anxious about public speaking to enjoying it without achieving a few intermediate steps. For example, I used to be anxious about public speaking because I had a particular attitude towards stammering in this setting. I first achieved the goal of being concerned but not anxious about stammering while I spoke in public and then continued to do this for a few years until I discovered that I enjoyed public speaking. The lesson to be learned from this is that your client may or may not end up enjoying public speaking. Still, they first need to achieve the intermediate goal of being un-anxiously concerned about doing so and then continue to speak in public to see if they enjoy it.

Once you have helped your client set a realistic problem-related goal, you may need to help them see the connection between their session goal and this problem-related goal. As a general rule, as the session goal is often equivalent to a problem-related solution, the repeated use of this solution will help your client to achieve their problem-related goal, as shown in the diagram below:

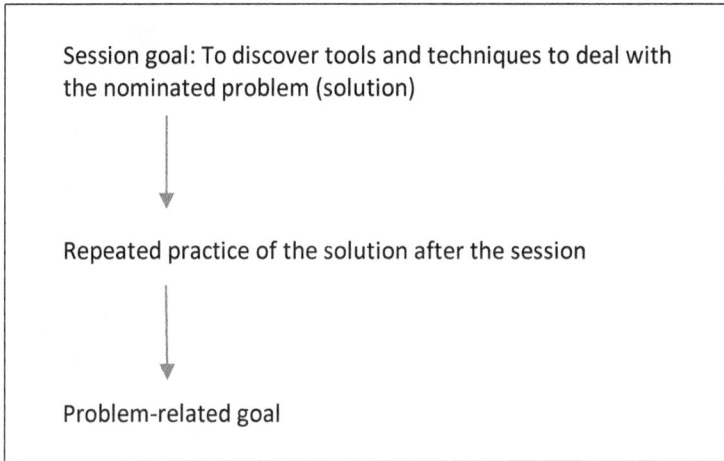

Session goal: To discover tools and techniques to deal with
the nominated problem (solution)

↓

Repeated practice of the solution after the session

↓

Problem-related goal

Focusing

In most cases in ONEplus therapy, you will need to help the client
select a focus for the session and then help them keep to the focus
you co-created.[13] This focus will be the issue or problem your
client has chosen to discuss with a view to, for example,
addressing it, understanding it or expressing their feelings about
it. In addition, if your client wants to use the session to make a
decision or resolve a dilemma, this will also form the focus of the
session. You need to have a few skills in your repertoire
regarding focusing. These are:

Agreeing on a Focus

Often, your client will indicate what they want to focus on in the
session. Thus, they may indicate this on the pre-session form that
you may send them in advance of the session, designed to help
them prepare for the session and to be returned to you to facilitate
your session preparation (see Chapter 7 and Appendix 7). If this

---

[13] The exception to this is when the client has chosen to talk in an unfettered
way and for you to listen to them.

is the case, you will need to check with them at the beginning phase of the session that this focus is still current. For example:

You:	I noticed on the form you completed and returned that you said you wanted to focus on your anxiety about giving a presentation to your colleagues. Is that right?
Client:	Yes, it is.
You:	Is that still the case?
Client:	Yes.

If this happens, then you can proceed. If the focus has changed, you can proceed as follows:

You:	Is that still the case?
Client:	Actually, no. I'd like to use the session to discuss something different.
You:	OK, that's fine. What do you want the focus of today's session to be?
Client:	I want to talk about dealing with my anger.
You:	OK. Your anger about what?
Client:	My anger about the way my boss treats us at work.

It may be the case that either on the pre-session preparation form or at the beginning of the session, your client indicates that they want to discuss more than one issue. Here is how to deal with this eventuality:

> *You:* I noticed on the form you completed and returned that you wanted to focus on your anxiety about giving a presentation to your colleagues and your anger about how your boss treats you and your colleagues at work. Is that right?
>
> *Client*: Yes, that's right.
>
> *You*: I will try to help you with both today, but if we can only deal with one, what issue do you want to select?
>
> *Client*: My anger about the way my boss treats us at work.

This issue now becomes the focus of the session. Once the two of you have discussed this issue, and the client has something to take away from the session that they can implement, the two of you need to decide whether you have sufficient time to discuss the second issue. If so, you can do so. If not, the client can choose to come back to discuss the second issue at another ONEplus therapy should they wish to do so.

Sometimes when the client has more than two issues to deal with, you can ask them to choose the one they wish to focus on, or you can help them identify a theme that links the issues. If you find one, you can offer the client an opportunity to focus on the theme. Here is an example of this:

> *You:* You listed three issues you wanted to discuss with me. The only way we can do this today is to see if there is a theme that links all three and work with this theme. OK?
>
> *Client:* OK.
>
> *You*: So, the three issues are fear of criticism, feelings of low self-esteem and a sense of shame when you show weakness. When you think about these three issues, can you see any theme that links all three?

Client: Well, I think it's low self-esteem.

You: OK, Shall we focus on low self-esteem and see if we can bring the other two issues into the picture where relevant?

Client: Yes.

Working with themes can be complex, so I suggest you postpone dealing with them until you have developed your confidence as a ONEplus therapist in focusing on and working with specific issues.

Maintaining a Focus

In *ordinary* conversation, it is a human tendency to move from topic to topic. In therapeutic conversation, as a ONEplus therapist, your task is to help your client stay with one topic and only move to another if there is sufficient time to do so and if you and your client have satisfactorily concluded your work on the first topic.

You can help a client maintain focus by gently guiding them back to the agreed focus once they have begun to stray from it. However, sometimes such gentle guidance has no effect, and you need to interrupt the client.

Interrupting your client

Interrupting your client is an important skill, the purpose of which is to help you and your client to maintain your agreed therapeutic focus. Here are the steps that I recommend you take when executing this skill.

1. Give a rationale for interrupting your client 'Sometimes, I may need to interrupt you if you move away from the focus we agreed on so we can get back on track.'

2. Ask for permission
   'Is it OK if I do this?'

3. Ask the client for advice about how to interrupt them best
   'From your perspective, how can I best interrupt you?'

Checking with the Client that the Focus Is Still Relevant

Even if a client is keeping to the agreed focus, it is good practice to check with them occasionally to see if they are discussing something they want to discuss. If they decide they are not discussing what is important to them, then if there is time, encourage them to change the focus to something more meaningful.

Responding to a Change of Topic

If you notice that your client has changed topic, you need to respond to this to understand the nature of this change. It may mean that you need to bring the client back to the agreed focus. By contrast, it may mean that you need to make the changed topic the new focus.

Being Clear in Your Communications and Clarifying Your Client's Communications

A general core skill in ONEplus therapy is being clear in what you say to your client and being clear about what your client says to you. If either of you misunderstands one another and moves forward based on such misunderstanding, this compromises the session's outcome.

Being Clear in What You Say to Your Client and Asking Them for Feedback

ONEplus therapy trainees differ in how clear they are when they counsel their trainee colleagues in peer counselling sessions. One of my primary tasks as a ONEplus therapy trainer is to give you feedback on how clear you are when offering your trainee colleague help in peer counselling.

When you are working with your clients in ONEplus therapy, it is good practice to record your sessions,[14] and while you are listening back to your work, ask yourself how clearly you have expressed yourself and how you could have been clearer in what you said to your client. Also, listen for occasions when you checked with your client whether they understood what you said. It is one thing improving the clarity of your communications from your perspective, but the critical issue is whether you are being clear to your client. The best way to answer this question is to ask your client about their understanding of what you have been saying to them in the session. Based on client feedback, you can clarify or change what you said until you and your client agree.

In checking my client's understanding of what I say to them in ONEplus therapy, I say things like:

- 'I'm not sure I have been clear in what I have been saying to you. Can you put that into your own words?'
- 'What's your understanding of what I have just said? I'm not sure if I have been clear.'
- 'You seem puzzled. It looks like I haven't been clear. Can I check that with you? What did you hear me say?'

It is important that you note that in each of the above interventions, I have stressed that I may not have been clear in what I have said to a client. The onus to communicate clearly in ONEplus therapy is on me, and I am transparent with my clients when I think I have failed to do so. I am also keen to avoid the client thinking I am testing them.

While being clear in what you say to your client is vital throughout the session, it is crucial in the following areas.

---

[14] Of course, this will be with the expressed permission of your clients.

Being clear about what ONEplus therapy is and what it is not

When you are called upon to tell a client about the nature of ONEplus therapy, it is vital that you do so with precise clarity. If need be, it is necessary for you to be clear about what ONEplus therapy isn't as well as what it is. As an exercise, I suggest you pair up with a trainee colleague, and, in your own words, each tells the other about what ONEplus therapy is and isn't.

Being clear about what you can and can't do in ONEplus therapy

If your client discloses an unrealistic expectation about what they hope to get from ONEplus therapy, it is vital that you are clear with them about what you can and cannot help them with. Here is an example:

Therapist:	What would you like to achieve from our conversation today?
Client:	I have a gambling problem and would like to get rid of this problem.
Therapist:	And you would like to achieve this by the end of the session?
Client:	Yes.
Therapist:	Well, I can't promise to help you do that. However, I can help both of us understand your problem and see how you can best tackle it going forward. Would you be interested in that?

It is vital that you do not tell your client what you can't do without telling them what you can do. Otherwise, they will end the session demoralised.

Being clear about your intended therapeutic strategies

ONEplus therapy is based on the client deciding what help is best for them. This means that if you have some suggestions about what might be helpful to the client in the session, then it is important that you are clear with the client about these therapeutic strategies, their purpose and what they involve for your client. Making yourself clear about these issues will enable your client to make an informed decision about them.

Being clear about any concepts you use

ONEplus therapists need to think carefully about using therapeutic concepts with clients, particularly if these ideas are in everyday use. For example, you might use the term 'acceptance' with your client, but do they know what you mean by it? Thus, you need to explain what you mean by the term 'acceptance' the first time you employ it. Here is an example:

Me: So, instead of trying to eliminate your anxious feelings, would it make sense to accept them?

Client: I am not sure.

Me: Would you like me to explain what I mean by acceptance here?

Client: Yes, please.

Me: Well, for me, it has three components. First, you acknowledge the existence of your anxious feelings. Second, you are clear with yourself that you don't like feeling anxious and would prefer not to feel this way. Third, you recognise you don't have to meet your preference in this respect. What would happen if you accepted your anxious feelings by this definition rather than trying to eliminate them?

Client:	I would find that very helpful.
Me:	In what way?
Client:	I would not be fighting with myself. Doing so tends to increase my anxiety, not decrease it.

Being clear about any explanations you give

While Socratic questioning actively involves your client in the process of ONEplus therapy, this way of questioning does not work with all clients. In this case, you may need to give your client short didactic explanations of ideas, points and other issues. Working didactically is sometimes necessary, even with clients who can resonate with Socratic work, since occasionally they may not grasp a point from your questioning.

When you give explanations in ONEplus therapy, keep them as short as possible, be as clear as possible, and check your client's understanding of what you have said. If it is necessary for you to give a lengthy explanation of a point, provide it in understandable 'chunks' of information and check your client's understanding along the way.

Being clear about what further help is available to your client

As I have mentioned several times in this book, more help is available to your client in ONEplus therapy. As such, it is vital that you make clear to your client *what* help is available to them should they want it, *who* will provide such help, *how* they can access it, and *how long* they will have to wait for it. Suppose you work in an agency that provides ONEplus therapy and other forms of therapy delivery. In that case, it is vital that the agency provides its relevant personnel with current waiting times[15] for all these forms of help.

Therapist: Before we finish today, as I see it, there are three ways forward. First, you can decide that you have got the help you wanted today and don't need any more. Second, you can decide you need more help, and we can discuss your options. Third, you can reflect on what we have discussed today, digest it, implement the takeaways and see what happens before deciding in the future whether to access more help. Each of these ways forward is perfectly fine. Which way forward best suits you?

Client: I found today helpful and will implement the takeaways. However, I would like some more help, if that's OK?

Therapist: OK. We offer three forms of help here. First, you can have another ONEplus therapy session with me or with a colleague of mine. There is a 5-day wait for such an appointment. Second, you can have a block of six counselling sessions with a colleague or me There is a 21-day wait for that to start. Finally, you can transfer to ongoing counselling, but I don't do this work at the agency. So, it will be with a colleague of mine. There is a six-week wait for that.

Client: Do I have to decide now?

Therapist: Not at all. Take as much time as you need. When you decide, call the agency's number, and let them know your preferred way forward.

---

[15] In general, clients are not interested in where they are on a waiting list for therapeutic help. They are interested, however, in how long they have to wait for such help.

Clarifying What Your Client Says to You

Clarity is important in two ways in ONEplus therapy. As discussed and demonstrated above, it is vital for you to be clear in your communications with your client. Equally important is that you are clear about your client's communications with you. If you are in doubt about this, then it is crucial that you check your understanding of what your client is saying. If you don't understand something they have said, you need to be transparent and say so. You need to be clear about what your client says to you in several crucial areas.

Clarifying your client's understanding of ONEplus therapy

Unless your client understands ONEplus therapy and what it can offer, their failure to understand it must be addressed immediately. If you do not do so, you will proceed with ONEplus therapy without your client's informed consent, which is unethical. You may also be providing them with help they do not want or failing to provide them with help that they do want.

There are a few ways to discover your client's understanding of ONEplus therapy, and I will discuss these in Chapter 8.

Clarifying what help the client wants from you

While most clients access ONEplus therapy because they want help with an emotional or behavioural problem with which they are stuck, this is not the only type of help that you can offer them. In Chapter 2, I reviewed these different types of help. Here is how you can clarify what help your clients want from you:

Therapist:	What's your understanding of the purpose of our conversation today?
Client:	It's to help me with an issue I have. You will try and help me by the end of the session, but I can have more help if I need it.
Therapist:	Yes, exactly. What type of help are you looking for?
Client:	I am not sure. I am confused about the nature of my problem.
Therapist:	So, would you like me to help you to get some clarity about the problem?
Client:	That would be good.
Therapist:	If you were clear about the problem, how would that be helpful to you?
Client:	If I were clear about it, I would help myself.
Therapist:	OK. Shall we go forward on the understanding that I will help you to become clear about the problem you are facing and that if you need more help after that, you can request it?
Client:	Yes.

Clarifying what the client wants to achieve from the session

The most salient aspect of ONEplus therapy concerns what your client wants to take from the session. This is known as the session goal. Understanding the client's session goal helps you to shape your thinking and influences your behaviour in the session. It is vital that you are clear about what the client wants in this respect. This also involves you helping the client to be clear in this respect, for clients are often vague or general about their session goal. Here is an example of how to gain such clarity:

Therapist: What would you like to achieve by the end of the session?

Client: I don't want to be as anxious as I am

Therapist: So, you still want to be anxious, but not as anxious as you are?

[*The client recognises that anxiety is problematic and indicates that they want to feel less of it. The therapist clarifies this.*]

Client: Well, I'd rather not be anxious at all.

Therapist: I get that. For me, when people are anxious, they face a threat. Does that make sense?

[*The therapist uses an opportunity to link threat and anxiety.*]

Client: Yes, my threat has to do with being rejected.

[*The client tells the therapist that the threat is being rejected.*]

Therapist: So, you are anxious about the prospect of being rejected.

[*The therapist clarifies that the client is anxious about being rejected.*]

Client: Yes.

Therapist: How would you like to deal with rejection?

[*Here, the therapist asks the client about their problem-related goal.*[16]]

Client: Good question. I've never really thought about that. I guess I don't want to be rejected.

[*The client states a goal that can't be achieved, as noted by the therapist in the following response.*]

---

[16] See Chapter 2 for a discussion about a problem-related goal and a session goal.

Therapist: Of course, you don't. I want to ensure you are never rejected, but is that possible?

Client: No, of course not.

Therapist: So, would you like to figure out a healthier way of dealing with rejection than anxiety?

[*Here, the therapist invites the client to see if there is a healthier response to rejection than anxiety.*]

Client: That would be great.

Therapist: Can I share a possibility with you?

Client: Of course.

Therapist: If I helped you to feel non-anxiously concerned about the prospect of being rejected rather than anxious about it, would you be interested in working towards that goal?

[*Here, the therapist could have first asked the client what they thought a healthy response to rejection was before offering their opinion.*]

Client: That would be great.

Therapist: I can't promise to do all of that today, but we could make a start and see what achieving that goal would involve. Perhaps we could also plan for you to implement that solution in your life. Would that be a good goal for the session?

[*Here, the therapist is distinguishing between the problem-related goal (non-anxious concern) and the session goal (finding a solution that the client could then implement in the service of reaching that problem-related goal) and offers to help the client achieve the latter by the end of the session.*]

Client: Absolutely

Tools and techniques. When people state their session goals for ONEplus therapy, they often say they seek 'tools and techniques' to help them cope with their nominated problems. This is how I tend to respond to such requests.

Windy:	What would you like to take from this session that would make a meaningful difference to you?
Client:	I'd like to learn some tips and techniques to help with my anxiety.
Windy:	What tips and techniques did you have in mind?
Client:	I'm not sure. I was hoping you would tell me.
Windy:	OK. Do you think it's best for us first to understand the factors that explain your anxiety, or can we dispense with such understanding and go straight to a discussion of tools and techniques?
Client:	I think we need to understand my anxiety first.
Windy:	So, let's start by understanding your anxiety, and based on that understanding, we can discuss how you can best address your anxiety. Does that make sense?
Client:	Yes.

In such cases, I help clients see that the choice of self-help methods (tools and techniques) must first be grounded in understanding their problem.

Clarifying your client's understanding of their problem and how it can best be tackled

Clients in ONEplus therapy vary significantly regarding their understanding of their problem and how it can best be tackled. Your main task here is to clarify what they know and offer them the opportunity to understand better their problem and what can be done about it. If they accept this opportunity, it is important that you stress that you will be offering them your view of these matters and that different therapists have different views.

Clarifying any words and phrases your client uses that you don't understand

It often happens in ONEplus therapy that a client will say something you don't understand. When this happens, you need to check your understanding with them and help them to be clearer if necessary. Here is an example.

Client: I want to feel OK whenever I get rejected for a job I applied for.

Therapist: What do you mean by 'OK' here?

Client: I mean, I don't want to be bothered by it.

Therapist: So, that is what OK means for you – not to be bothered about getting a job rejection. I'm a bit confused. Not being bothered seems to mean for you the absence of emotion about such rejection, whereas OK has the connotation of you feeling positive about it.

Client: Well, I want to feel nothing about getting rejected.

Therapist: I am not sure I can help you to do that. Can I explain?

Client: OK.

Therapist: Would you prefer to get the job you applied for or be rejected?

Client: To get the job, obviously.

Therapist:	Right, so it matters to you and when something matters to you, like getting a job you applied for, you will have negative feelings if you get rejected. Do you follow me?
Client:	Yes, as getting a job is important to me, I will have negative feelings if my application is rejected.
Therapist:	So, that's why I can't help you not to feel bothered or to feel OK about being rejected for a job. What help I can provide depends on how you feel and respond to job rejections. Shall we begin there?
Client:	That sounds sensible.

Having discussed the general core skills you will need to develop as a ONEplus therapist, in the following chapter, I will turn my attention to the issue of having your practice of ONEplus therapy supervised as part of the training course.

4

Having Your Practice Supervised

In the previous two chapters. I outlined what you need to know about ONEplus therapy and the general skills you need to develop to prepare yourself to be a practitioner of this form of therapy delivery. As mentioned in the previous chapter, in developing general and specific skills related to ONEplus therapy practice, it is important that you practise these skills while being a therapist and a client with your trainee colleagues. This will be done in front of your training cohort, and your trainer will offer you feedback based on what they observed during the session. I referred you to Appendix 3 for a list of the relevant skills that your trainer will be looking for and giving you feedback on

However, the most important part of your preparation is to practise ONEplus therapy with clients and have this practice supervised. There are two primary ways of doing this. First, audio- or video-record your work with your clients and present these recordings for supervision. Second, discuss your work with your supervisor focusing on the issues your work has posed for you. In effect, it is best to have supervision that offers both.

Having Recordings of Your Client Work
Supervised

ONEplus therapy is particularly suited to be recorded as you will only see many of your clients once. Therefore, your supervisor can listen to your work with such clients from beginning to end. In my experience, therapists can be reluctant to make recordings of their ONEplus therapy sessions.

Thus, you may be:

- Reluctant to have your actual work commented on by others.
- Reluctant to ask clients for permission to record sessions.
- Self-critical when watching or listening to one's work.

Experienced therapists tend to be more reluctant about making recordings than their less experienced colleagues. The latter group tend to accept their trainee ONEplus therapy status more than the former. If you are reluctant to make and play recordings of your sessions to your supervisor (either in individual or group supervision), then it is important that you address it. On your training course, it would be a relevant topic to discuss at one of your peer counselling sessions when you are a client.

Obtain Your Client's Informed Consent for Having Their Session Recording

If you plan to record your sessions with your clients, it goes without saying that you need to get their informed consent to do so. This means that you need to explain to them the reasons why you wish to make such recordings and who will listen to them. Here is what I suggest to my ONEplus therapy supervisees.

- Tell your client that you wish to record your session and make clear the method of recording (e.g. audio or video).

- Tell them that the purpose of the recording is for you to play it with your supervisor, who will give you feedback on your skills so that you can develop yourself as a ONEplus therapist. If you have group supervision, explain who else will be viewing or listening to the recording.

- Offer them the session recording so they can review it later.

- If you want a written transcript of the session, tell them that the purpose of doing so is for you to review the session later. Also, if you want your supervisor to give you feedback on the transcript, inform your client about this. Also, offer them a copy of the transcript.

- Ask your client for permission for the above, preferably in writing.

Methods of Having Recordings Supervised

There are several ways in which you can have your recordings supervised.

Individual supervision

In individual supervision, you meet with your supervisor on your own, either face-to-face or online.

1. You can meet with your supervisor and play segments of the recording for supervisory comments. You probably don't have time to play the entire session and get supervision.

2. You can send the recording to your supervisor, let them listen, and then meet briefly with them to get their supervisory comments.

3. You can send your supervisor the session transcript, have them give you their supervisory comments in writing on the transcript and then meet with them to discuss their feedback.

The advantage of individual supervision of recorded ONEplus therapy sessions is that your supervisor's attention will solely be on your work.

Group supervision

In group supervision, you meet with your supervisor and others training to become ONEplus therapists. The minimum amount of time each supervisee in the group should have is 30 mins, so the length of the group will vary according to its membership. Given this, you will only have time to present a few segments from the recorded ONEplus therapy session at each group supervision session.

The advantage of group supervision of recorded ONEplus therapy sessions is that you can learn from your supervisor's comments about your practice and the practice of your group supervisee colleagues.

Discussing Your Work

When the supervision of your ONEplus therapy practice is focused on discussing your work rather than playing recordings of that work, you will probably focus on a session with which you experienced difficulty.[17] Here, your supervisor will explore with you the difficulty you faced and what it was about the situation that was difficult for you. Then, they will help you to address the difficulty. Let me provide an example:

Supervisor:	What would you like to discuss today?
Supervisee:	I want to discuss a student I saw a few days ago with whom I struggled.
Supervisor:	Please tell me a little about the student, and then we can focus on what you struggled with.

---

[17] While you will most often discuss a 'case' with which you had difficulty, it is important that for balance that your supervisor also asks you to discuss a 'case' which went well.

Supervisee: The student was sent by his tutor to the ONEplus therapy service, and he wanted to discuss whether he should continue his course or start a new course. He is a second-year medical student but is not enjoying it, nor does he want to become a doctor. He wants to study Physics which was his best subject at school and which he really enjoys.

Supervisor: It sounds like he has already made up his mind.

Supervisee: That's what I thought, but when I put that to him, he said that all the men in his family are doctors going back generations, and he doesn't want to disappoint anyone.

Supervisor: So, how did you respond?

Supervisee: That's when I started to panic. His issue seemed enormous, and I kept thinking about how am I going to help him in one session.

Supervisor: It sounds like you let go of the single-session mindset at that point.

Supervisee: Exactly.

Supervisor: What did you do?

Supervisee: First, I went quiet, and then I started talking about organisations he could contact, which deal with similar situations.

Supervisor: How did he respond to that?

Supervisee: Well, I think he was a little nonplussed. I guessed he thought I would help him with this issue, not refer him elsewhere. However, he thanked me for my help at the end and said it was good to talk.

Supervisor: Having had the opportunity to reflect on and discuss the issue with me, what is your understanding of your difficulty with this student?

Supervisee: I assumed I could not help him with his conflict because it seemed so big a problem and was rooted in cultural issues.

Supervisor: And if you revisit the situation from a ONEplus therapy mindset, what would you do differently?

Supervisee: I would ask the client if he wants to discuss the issue with me and if he does, what does he want to take away from our conversation?

Supervisor: And you would have done so, even if the problem seemed big and rooted in cultural issues?

Supervisee: Yes, it is what we learned in our ONEplus therapy training. Let the client decide what they want to discuss in the session. I decided we wouldn't discuss the issue because I thought it was too big a problem. I never asked him what he wanted to do. It seems so obvious in retrospect.

Supervisor: Do you think people who have been steeped in the traditional therapy mindset, find it easy to switch to the ONEplus therapy mindset?

Supervisee. Not at all. Some trainees and I formed a WhatsApp group[18] to discuss our difficulties with ONEplus therapy and getting support from one another and the Number 1 difficulty is struggling to maintain the ONEplus therapy mindset throughout the session.

[18] It is made clear to trainees on the ONEplus therapy training course that client work should not be discussed on such online group. The emphasis should be on providing mutual support.

Supervisor:	From my perspective as a supervisor of ONEplus therapy trainees, there are three issues for you and your trainee colleagues who struggle with maintaining the ONEplus therapy for the duration of the session to address. Can I list them individually, and then we can discuss them one at a time?
Supervisee:	Sure.
Supervisor:	The first issue involves you keeping a note when you find yourself returning to the conventional therapy mindset in a ONEplus therapy session and reflecting on what led you to do that. OK?
Supervisee:	Makes perfect sense. Can I bring issues that I am not sure about to supervision like I did today?
Supervisor:	Of course. The second issue relates to what you did today. You stood back and responded to your conventional therapy thinking, and you could do this outside of supervision too. OK?
Supervisee:	OK
Supervisor:	The final issue concerns catching yourself reverting to the conventional therapy mindset and responding quickly to it you can maintain the ONEplus therapy mindset during the session. What do you think of this final issue?
Supervisee:	Easier said than done.
Supervisor:	Indeed, but it can be done, and maybe we should focus initially on the first two issues.
Supervisor:	Makes sense.

As you can tell, particularly at the end of the transcript, the supervisor adopts an educational stance and offers the supervisee a framework to deal with a common issue in ONEplus therapy: how to respond to conventional therapy thinking with ONEplus therapy thinking.

Discussing Personal Struggles with ONEplus Therapy

Our field generally agrees that supervision and personal therapy are different therapeutic activities. However, it sometimes occurs that the supervisee has a personal struggle which affects their work as a ONEplus therapist and wants a forum to discuss this in supervision. This is fine as long as the supervisor and supervisee have clear boundaries[19] concerning what constitutes personal therapy and a discussion of personal struggle that a supervisee has in their ONEplus therapy practice.

In my experience, the following two issues are those with which many ONEplus therapists struggle.[20]

Not doing more for the client

ONEplus therapists may struggle with not offering the client more help. Some deal with this struggle by emailing clients a long list of links and resources they can access. Others respond by emphasising the 'more help is available' option when reviewing the end-of-session helping options with clients. Therapists who struggle with this issue and do neither of the above often experience guilt about not providing as much help as they think they should.

Here, the supervisor should engage the supervisee in a conversation about which therapeutic value has primacy in this situation: the client determining how much therapy they want or the therapist determining how much therapy the client needs.

---

[19] If the supervisor is unsure about this, they need to discuss it with a trusted colleague rather than decide independently.

[20] In this section, I will only discuss personal struggles that people have with ONEplus therapy, not other forms of therapy delivery.

Difficulty letting go of one's initial training

Practitioners can practise ONEplus therapy from a variety of different therapeutic orientations. However, therapists must be informed by the ONEplus therapy mindset for this to happen. Thus, practising ONEplus therapy is impossible if one favours, for example, a protocol-driven form of cognitive behaviour therapy. The therapist can be informed by some ideas related to this approach, but they can't import the entire approach into ONEplus therapy. In my view, it is the therapist who tries to hold tightly to their initial training and attempts to practise ONEplus therapy accordingly who really struggles. It is as if they have been told how to practise therapy, are committed to that view and can't set it aside.

Here, the supervisor needs to engage the therapist in a conversation about the importance of using therapy mindsets for different forms of therapy delivery. For example, using a ONEplus therapy mindset for ONEplus therapy and a protocol-driven therapy mindset for protocol-driven therapy. If the therapist cannot resolve this struggle, the practice of ONEplus therapy may not be for them. Nobody should be compelled to practise ONEplus therapy when they don't want to do so.

Case Discussion Formats

There are two main formats of discussion-based supervision: (i) Individual case discussion and (ii) Group-based case discussion.

Individual case discussion of ONEplus therapy

When a therapist contracts with a ONEplus therapy supervisor, it is vital that they discuss what general issues will form the basis of that supervision. As shown above, perhaps the most critical issue that needs to be discussed concerns the therapist's practice of ONEplus therapy. When I supervise an individual, I make clear that they can bring both their difficulties in their practice of ONEplus therapy and work with which they are pleased. If they have 50 minutes for such supervision, then they may well be time to discuss both.

In addition, the therapist can discuss their personal struggles in the practice of ONEplus therapy. Individual supervision is the best format for discussing such struggles when the person would not choose to disclose in ONEplus therapy group discussion-based supervision.

Group case discussion of ONEplus therapy

Whenever I run discussion-based group supervision, which tends to be held monthly, I recommend that the number of supervisees in the group is calculated by the formula that for every group member, 30 minutes are allocated. Thus, a 90-minute supervision group has three members, a two-hour group has four members and so forth. It is vital that with this arrangement, supervision time (i.e. 30 minutes) is spent with each supervisee. It is best if a supervisee prepares themself for supervision. I explain that they can bring a case where they experienced a difficulty, one where they did well or a more general struggle that they have with practising ONEplus therapy. During the 30 minutes allocated to each supervisee, time should be made for the other attending supervisees to give feedback to the presenting supervisee so that a sense of group trust and cohesion can be developed.

Combining Both Forms of Supervision

So far, I have discussed supervision (individual or group) as either based on recordings of ONEplus therapy or case discussion of this work. Combining these two forms of ONEplus therapy supervision is the best practice, in my view. When the focus is on helping the supervisee to develop their ONEplus therapy skills, then listening to and commenting on recordings of sessions is the supervision mode of choice. When the supervisee wants to discuss a more general difficulty with a client or their struggle with the ONEplus therapy mindset or with the general practice of ONEplus therapy, then discussion-based supervision is best.

That said, when the supervisee wishes to discuss a difficulty with a specific client, they can be encouraged to bring in a recorded segment of the session in which the difficulty showed up. This means that not only can the supervisee's difficulty with the client be discussed, but the possible contribution of what they said to the difficulty they had can also be listened to and suggestions made concerning alternative ways of responding to the client.

Bringing the ONEplus Therapy Mindset to Supervision

While the ONEplus therapy mindset was designed to underpin the practice of the therapy, the mindset can also be applied, with suitable modifications to other therapeutic endeavours such as supervision,

The Supervisor's Mindset

Although the supervision of ONEplus therapy tends to be ongoing, some supervisors bring a ONEplus therapy mindset to supervision, whether individual or group, and whether recordings of sessions or case discussions are the focus of supervision. For example, Rycroft (2018) outlined a Single-Session Supervision (SSS) framework which has the following structure:

- *Context setting, connecting and contracting*
  If the supervisee and supervisor have not met before, there is a period where mutual expectations are shared, exceptions to confidentiality are made clear, and a contract between the two is agreed upon. Then, the supervisee shares information about their working

context. Finally, a goal is agreed upon for the supervision session.[21]

- *Finding a focus*
  After goal-setting, the supervisor and supervisee create a focus (for example, a particular difficulty that the supervisee has with a client they wish to discuss). This is named so that both know what they are working with

- *Staying on track*
  During the supervisee's discussion of the issues relevant to the focus, the supervisor checks that the former is still discussing what they want to discuss.

- *Investigating attempted solutions*
  The supervisor asks the supervisee to tell what they have tried that has been helpful with the difficulty and what has not been helpful. The supervisor asks the supervisee to nominate suggested solutions based on what they know about themself (e.g. clinical strengths) and the client (what the client is likely to respond well to).[22]

- *Reviewing/Transition*
  At this point, the supervisor asks the supervisee if there is anything that they haven't said about the issue that they would like to say before hearing the supervisor's view.

- *Reflection*
  The supervisor offers their view based on what has been said and the supervisee's goal for the supervision session in mind. The supervisor ensures that a balance between support and challenge is maintained.

---

[21] If the supervisor and supervisee have met before then the session starts with goal-setting.
[22] These possible solutions may be applied when the supervisee sees the client again. If not, the possible solution can be implemented if the supervisee encounters a similar difficulty in the future.

- *Hearing the supervisee's feedback*
  The supervisor asks the supervisee for feedback on their expressed view and invites the supervisee to mention anything that they are uncomfortable with. If so, this is discussed.
- *Checking in and closure*
  The supervisor asks the supervisee whether they got what they hoped to get from the session and the key points they will take away and implement. Before closing, the supervisor invites the supervisee to say anything on the issue that they would like to say and haven't yet and to ask the supervisor anything that they would like to ask.

The Supervisee's Mindset

You can, if you wish, also bring a ONEplus therapy mindset to supervision. Here is what this might involve:

- Consider what you want to achieve from the supervision session and communicate this to your supervisor.

- Suggest and agree upon a focus with your supervisor.

- Prepare all relevant information before the session and tell this to your supervisor.

- Together with your supervisor, look for something new that could make a difference and help you to achieve what you want from the supervision session. This may be a new perspective, a new skill or a way of overcoming an obstacle to adopting the ONEplus therapy mindset.

- Plan to implement whatever new learning you derive from the session.

In the next part of this book, I will discuss laying the foundations for the practice of ONEplus therapy.

Part II

Laying the Foundations for ONEplus Therapy

PREAMBLE

In Part I of this book, I discussed what you need to do to prepare yourself to become a ONEplus therapist. Having prepared yourself in the knowledge, mindset, skills and supervised practice elements of the work, you are ready to practise either in your independent practice or in the agency which employs you. However, it is important to remember that however well-prepared you are, you need to lay the foundations for your practice of ONEplus therapy by doing two things: (a) providing information for potential clients and (b) developing relationships with stakeholders. I will consider both these issues in Part II of this book.

5

Providing Information for Potential Clients

You may have prepared yourself fully to be an excellent practitioner of ONEplus therapy. Still, unless your potential clientele knows about this form of therapy delivery, then you will not be able to practise it since nobody will request it. So, a vital part of laying the foundations of your ONEplus therapy practice is disseminating it to your potential clientele. I will deal with this topic in two parts. First, I will assume that you are working in an agency that has decided to offer ONEplus therapy to the client population that they serve. Second, I will assume that you are working in independent practice and have decided to offer ONEplus therapy as a form of therapy delivery alongside other forms.

Disseminating ONEplus Therapy in an Agency

This section will discuss two examples of how an agency has disseminated ONEplus therapy to its potential clientele on its website. I will make appropriate comments along the way.

An NHS Talking Therapy Service (UK)

'Help Here'[23] displays 'Single-Session Therapy'[24] on their website as a tab. When a person clicks the tab, it sends them to a separate page under the heading, 'Single-session therapy'. This is what is described:

SINGLE-SESSION THERAPY (SST)

'Help Here' now offers Single-Session Therapy to patients, subject to suitability.

[*The fact that the agency mentions 'subject to suitability' is problematic because one of the fundamental principles of SST/ONEplus therapy, which is that the client decides what kind of help they want to access rather than the agency.*]

This means we can offer you a single session quickly, usually in the next week.

The aim is to help you get as much as possible in a single session with the understanding that more help is available if needed.

[*This is very much in line with the nature of SST/ONEplus therapy as described in this book.*]

In the session, your therapist would help you focus on the issue that you are most bothered about and encourage you to address it effectively.

Your role is to come to the session prepared to focus on that one issue and work with them to see if you and they can come up with a meaningful solution that you can take forward into your own life.

---

[23] To preserve this agency's privacy, I will refer to it as 'Help Here'.
[24] As the agency refers to Single-Session Therapy on its website, I will use that term when presenting and commenting on what they say.

[*This section stresses the importance of the client coming to the session prepared with a focus (see Chapter 8) and describes well the collaborative nature of SST/ONEplus therapy.*]

The goal of the session is to help you to take the first steps towards doing this rather than solving the problem in its entirety.

[*This section sets realistic expectations about what the client is likely to achieve from SST/ONEplus therapy.*]

We will follow up this session with a short phone review, usually in about four weeks. At that time, you may say that you have had all the help you need at this stage, or you might ask to get treatment from 'Help Here' therapists in the usual manner, in which case it would be made available to you.

[*It is common in agencies to telephone clients to see if they need more help; two to three weeks is the usual gap. Four weeks seems a little long. Also, the client can't nominate having another single session as a way of having more help. Perhaps the reason is explained by the offer of getting 'treatment in the usual manner' from 'Help Here' therapists, which implies that SST is not an integral part of what the agency offers. It is outside of the usual.*]

Find out more about Single-Session Therapy by watching this short video.

[*This is a video that I created:*
https://www.youtube.com/watch?v=wIcuOVOABRw&t=22s]

Please bear in mind that 'Help Here' cannot offer walk-in sessions as described but can offer appointments for SST soon.
Do you think this would be helpful for you?
If you would like a single session therapy at 'Help Here', use the self-refer link in the menu at the top of the page AND MENTION ON THE FORM THAT YOU WOULD LIKE SST.

You will then get a call TO ASSESS SUITABILITY and then a single session appointment, currently by video or phone.

[*As I mentioned above, this agency has determined that it will decide whether to offer a client SST/ONEplus therapy rather than leaving it for the client to decide.*]

Single-Session Therapy can help with a range of issues, including low mood, anxiety, relationship issues and Covid-related concerns. It is not intended for those in crisis – if you are in urgent need of help or feeling suicidal, please visit -
_____ .

[*While it is not strictly the case that SST/ONEplus therapy is not intended for those who are in crisis or are suicidal, open access, walk-in services would be the best forum for such clients. 'Help Here' offers SST/ONEplus therapy by appointment. As the agency says, an appointment can result in a single session occurring within a week after the appointment has been made. It is understandable, therefore, for the agency to state that SST/ONEplus therapy by appointment is not suitable for those in crisis or who are suicidal.*]

A Relationships Counselling Agency (Australia)

On their website, 'Relate Better'[25] refers to ONEplus therapy as a 'Single-Session Consultation', and I will use their terminology when discussing this mode of therapy delivery as described on their website.

What is a Single-Session Consultation?

- A Single-Session Consultation (SSC) is an evidence-informed, client-focused counselling session. The focus of the session is on your greatest worry, challenge or difficulty and what you want to achieve from your

---

[25] To preserve this agency's privacy, I will refer to it as 'Relate Better'.

meeting. We aim for you to leave the session with some ideas or strategies to try out.

[*This is all fine, except the client*[26] *may not wish to discuss their 'greatest' worry, challenge or difficulty. I would suggest saying, 'The focus of the session is on the worry, challenge or difficulty you wish to discuss and what you want to achieve from our meeting. '*]

- Single-Session Consultations are suitable for individuals, couples or families. They can be facilitated by one practitioner or sometimes two. A single-session consultation involves a longer than usual counselling session and a follow-up phone call to discuss the next steps.

[*A few points to note here. (1) Family work is often facilitated by more than one therapist; (2). Single sessions are often longer than usual for couples and families but not necessarily for individuals.' I would have changed 'involves' to 'may involve'.*]

Why Should I Choose a Single-Session Consultation?
- People choose a Single-Session Consultation for different reasons. The sessions can help ensure you're getting the most out of your first, and sometimes only, session. Experience tells us that about half the time, people will come back for further counselling, while the rest are happy with one session. Both outcomes are okay. You are always welcome to return to 'Relate Better' if you need further assistance.

[*This is accurate concerning the 50% seeking further help figure. I particularly like the 'both outcomes are okay' statement.*]

---

[26] When I use the term 'client' in this section, this may refer to a person, a couple or a family.

- In a Single-Session Consultation, our practitioners aim to maximise your time by focusing on your greatest concern. Single-Session Consultations are appealing because they are collaborative and responsive; they focus on your key concerns and goals, and you and your practitioner work together on strategies for change.

[*I have already mentioned the problem with the emphasis on the client's greatest rather than nominated concern which may or not be the same. However, I like the rest of this statement which stresses the goal-directed and collaborative nature of the work.*]

For What Issues Can Single-Session Consultations be Helpful?
- Single-Session Consultations can be used for a wide range of issues. We work to help individuals, couples and families to improve their relationships and find ways to manage issues such as separation and divorce, grief and loss, mental health issues, life changes, family violence, managing emotions, parenting issues and managing stress.

[*This reflects the issues that 'Relate Better' clients tend to bring. Other agencies would include issues that their clients commonly seek help for.*]

- In fact, people attend Single-Session Consultations for the same reasons as ongoing counselling and other services. In a Single-Session Consultation, however, we can offer a contained and immediate response to your most pressing concern. While Single Session Consultations focus on your greatest concern, they can still be suitable for those with multiple and or complex issues. You may have a lot going on, but still find a single session to be helpful to you and your circumstances.

[*Once again. I would suggest replacing the phrases 'most pressing concern' and 'greatest concern' with the phrase 'nominated concern'. However, I like the mention that clients can bring the same issues to SSC that they bring to longer-term counselling, with the difference being that they will get a 'contained and immediate response' in the former. I particularly like that clients can get help in SSC even with multiple or complex issues.]*

What Does a Single Session Consultation Involve?

• Before you attend a session, you'll be sent a questionnaire to fill in to help your practitioner find out more about your main concerns and goals for the session. You'll need to complete and return this questionnaire when you attend your session.

[I don't like this for two reasons. First, it makes clear that the purpose of the completion pre-session questionnaire is to help the therapist be prepared for the session rather than helping the client prepare for the session so that they can get the most from it. Second, it does not make clear whether the filling-in and return of the form is advised or mandated. What if the client does not want to complete the form? Can they still have the session? Greater clarity on this point is needed.]

• After your session, your therapist will arrange a follow-up phone call to see how you're going and discuss options for further support. If you feel that the single session was sufficient and has met your needs, your practitioner will close your file with the understanding that you are welcome to re-contact 'Relate Better' at any time in the future.

[This is standard. However, greater clarity is needed concerning when the follow-up call will take place, although this will probably be made clear at the end of the session.]

Disseminating ONEplus Therapy in Independent Practice

In this section, I will present the information I have on my website about ONEplus and discuss a leaflet I have put together for clients.

Website

On my website, the following information appears about ONEplus therapy:

What is ONEplus Therapy?

ONEplus therapy occurs when you and I agree to meet for one session with the intention of me helping you to walk away from the session with the help you are looking for, which, when you implement it, will make a meaningful difference to your life. It is also important for you to realise that more help is available should you request it.

Is ONEplus Therapy for Me?

ONEplus therapy is for you if you are stuck with an emotional or behavioural problem and are looking for a way to get unstuck. It is not for you if you seek ongoing therapy to address your problems.

For Which Issues Can ONEplus Therapy be Helpful?

ONEplus therapy can help you address the same issues that can be addressed in other forms of therapy delivery. The difference is that in ONEplus therapy, we will work from moment one to help you to take away what you have come for on the issue you have chosen to discuss with me. Thus, in ONEplus therapy, I do not take a case history or carry out an extensive assessment of you and your problems.

Can I Prepare for ONEplus Therapy?

Once you decide to have ONEplus therapy, I will send you a contract to sign. On receipt, we will make an appointment.

Beforehand, I will send you a pre-session questionnaire to complete and return. While this is optional and not mandatory, the questionnaire is designed to help you prepare for the session so that you get the most from it. Sharing your questionnaire with me before the session also helps me prepare for the session.

What does ONEplus Therapy Involve?

At the beginning of the session, I will check that you understand the purpose of the session, and if so, I will help you to clarify what you want to take away from the session. We will then agree on a focus for the session, which is usually the issue for which you seek help. It is my responsibility to help us both keep to this focus. I will then help you to discover a potential solution to the problem and encourage you to rehearse it in the session to see if it is right for you. If so, I will help you develop a plan to implement the solution and clarify your takeaways from the session.

What Happens at the End of the Session?

At the end of the session, we will discuss the next steps. The options are (i) You conclude that you got what you came for and need no further help; (ii) You indicate that you would like some time to reflect on the session, put into practice what you learned and then decide if you need further help and iii) You decide that you would like further help which might include having another session, having an agreed block of sessions or opting for ongoing therapy. If, at the end of the session, we agree that you need more specialised help than I can provide, then I will help you find such help.

Is There Anything Else I Need to Know?

- At the moment, I am only offering ONEplus therapy online.
- With your permission, I will record the session and send you an audio recording of the session free of charge.
- If you want a written transcript, I can provide one at what it costs me to have it transcribed professionally.

Leaflet

Not all ONEplus therapists have a website, and not all clients consult therapists' websites for information about their services. Consequently, if you choose not to have a website or even if you choose to have one, I recommend that you develop a leaflet on ONEplus therapy for potential clients. You can send one to those enquiring about ONEplus therapy, and you can also send a number to be put on noticeboards of relevant places such as GP surgeries. See Appendix 2 for an example of a leaflet explaining ONEplus therapy that I devised and send out to potential clients interested in learning more about ONEplus therapy.

Responding Effectively to the Person's First Contact

When a person makes contact for any form of therapy, I believe they merit a prompt response from you if you work as an independent practitioner or from someone in the therapy agency who is accessible, attentive and knowledgeable.

Discover What Help-Seeking Mode a Person is in and Respond Accordingly

When a person contacts a therapist, they are in one of two modes: enquirer or applicant. When a person is in the enquirer mode, they seek the right approach and/or right therapist at a price they can afford (if in the private sector), but they have not decided whom they wish to consult. If they are in applicant mode, they have decided to see a particular therapist or seek help from a particular agency. The onus here is on the therapist or agency representative to judge whether they can help the person. If not, then an appropriate referral should be made. It should be noted that the person only becomes a client when the person has given their informed consent to proceed.

Outline Services

It is a good idea for the therapist (or agency representative) to outline what services are offered, including a thumbnail description of ONEplus therapy. Then the person can decide whether ONEplus therapy is appropriate for them and whether the therapist (or agency) is most suitable.

Explain the Process of ONEplus Therapy

Once the person has made contact, the therapist (or agency representative) should offer a more detailed explanation of the process of ONEplus therapy so that the person is better prepared for the next phase. Utilising an opening gambit offered by Hoyt, Rosenbaum and Talmon (1992: 69), the therapist might say: 'Many people who seek therapy find that a single session can help a lot. So if we are both ready to address your problem, then I'll do my best to help you get what you are looking for from therapy in that one session. If you need further help after that, then that is possible too. Is that something that you would like to pursue?'

*

In the next chapter, I will discuss the need for you to develop relationships with stakeholders if you work in independent practice or if you work in an agency.

6

Developing Relationships with Stakeholders

It is important to view the practice of ONEplus therapy in context, whether this be the context in which your independent practice is located or the context which frames the work of the therapy agency which employs you. When this contextual perspective is taken, it readily becomes apparent that there are a number of people who have an interest in the work that you do in your independent practice and in work done by the therapy agency with which you are associated. In this chapter, I refer to such people as stakeholders. I will focus on the relationships you need to build with these stakeholders if the ONEplus therapy arm of your practice and the agency's offering of this form of therapy delivery is to survive and even thrive.

Developing Relationships with Stakeholders in Independent Practice

If you are in independent practice, you did not have to liaise with anyone to set up this practice. However, since your practice's lifeblood is clients, you need to do something to get a steady stream of referrals. This means finding people who will refer to you. This is something that anyone faces in running an independent practice. However, given that you have decided to include ONEplus therapy in your therapy delivery and many people in the field will not be au fait with it, you face a challenge in finding ways to inform them of ONEplus therapy.

Who Are Your Stakeholders?

Your stakeholders will be professionals interested enough in what you do and, over time, sufficiently pleased with the results you achieve to continue referring clients to you. Stakeholders may include local GPs, other therapists who do not offer ONEplus therapy, and local mental health agencies willing to add your services to a list of resources clients may wish to consider.

How Can You Inform Stakeholders about ONEplus Therapy?

There are several ways in which you can inform stakeholders about ONEplus therapy. You can do so by holding meetings with them, giving them a short presentation about ONEplus therapy or sending them a leaflet about this form of therapy delivery. Of course, these are not mutually exclusive. Thus, you may send a stakeholder an explanatory leaflet about ONEplus therapy. In an accompanying letter or email, you can mention that you would be happy to meet informally with people working with the stakeholder to discuss ONEplus therapy in greater depth and answer any of their questions. You might also suggest giving them a more formal presentation about ONEplus therapy where you would and again answer any of their questions.

Leaflet

In the previous chapter, I briefly discussed a leaflet I send out to potential clients explaining the nature of ONEplus therapy (see Appendix 2). I suggested there that you devise your own leaflet to send out when people contact you and want more information about ONEplus therapy.

    You can devise a similar leaflet to send to stakeholders, which again outlines the nature of ONEplus therapy. Appendix 4 presents a leaflet I devised to send to stakeholders.

Meetings

You may suggest a meeting with stakeholders, or they may request to meet with you to learn more about ONEplus therapy and ask questions about it. These meetings are best held informally, in my experience, and allow you to have a conversation about ONEplus therapy with stakeholders. You do need to prepare yourself to answer a series of questions, most of which will be asked from a more conventional therapy mindset. For suggestions about responding to frequently asked questions (FAQs) about ONEplus therapy, I suggest you consult Dryden (2022a). The most common of these FAQs are as follows:

- Which clients are suitable and which clients are not suitable for ONEplus therapy?
- How can a productive therapy relationship be developed in one session?
- Which client problems can be addressed in ONEplus therapy and which can't?

Presentations

Giving a presentation to stakeholders when you are an independent practitioner is a good way to outline ONEplus therapy because you are in charge of what you present. As mentioned above, a meeting tends to be more informal and conversational, and thus, you may not be able to get across fully what you want to say. Giving a short PowerPoint presentation (no more than an hour) lets you decide what you want to present to inform your stakeholders about ONEplus therapy. You will still have to take questions at the end, so preparing to answer the frequently asked questions I listed above is vital.

Developing Relationships with Stakeholders in Therapy Agencies

The entire therapy agency must be thoroughly committed to ONEplus therapy for it to thrive in that agency. This does not happen overnight but is the result of many consultations involving all stakeholders, many of whom should ideally be involved in the decision to introduce ONEplus therapy into the agency, in the planning of how it is to be integrated into the agency and in its implementation by the agency.

ONEplus therapy was partly developed from the realisation that the modal number of sessions[27] clients attend in therapy agencies is '1' followed by '2', followed by '3', etc. (e.g., Brown & Jones, 2005). Previously, most clients in therapy agencies were offered a block of counselling sessions (usually six) even though many did not want so many sessions. So, ONEplus therapy was designed to help those who, if given the opportunity, could take what they wanted from a single therapy session, knowing that they could have more help if they requested it. This is the therapeutic *intention* of ONEplus therapy, to provide one session of therapy to those who want it and may not need any more sessions.

When ONEplus therapy is introduced into an agency, it has the *effect* of reducing waiting lists and waiting times for clients. When a therapy agency considers introducing ONEplus therapy to reduce waiting lists and waiting times for clients, it does so for administrative and not therapeutic reasons. This means the agency will not get the most out of what ONEplus therapy offers therapeutically. As such, eventually, ONEplus therapy will either be dropped from that agency or marginalised within it.

No matter who first comes up with the idea of introducing ONEplus therapy into a therapy agency, the following stakeholders should be consulted.

---

[27] The mode is the most frequently occurring number in a series.

Managers

Unless the agency's management team is committed to introducing ONEplus therapy into the suite of therapeutic services offered by the agency, then it will not happen. Suppose the agency's managers are also trained therapists. In that case, they will be concerned with the therapeutic reasons for introducing ONEplus therapy and how this form of therapy delivery can be integrated into the agency from a managerial perspective. If the managers are not trained therapists, they will mainly be concerned with this latter issue. On this point, managers will need to be satisfied that:

- The introduction of ONEplus therapy will improve services for clients.

- The agency's therapeutic team is committed to the introduction of ONEplus therapy.

- The introduction of ONEplus therapy into the agency will not hurt the other forms of therapy delivery.

- The overall management of the service will not be negatively impacted by the introduction of ONEplus therapy.

- The introduction of ONEplus therapy will not mean that additional therapists need to be recruited, or if it does mean this, then such appointments as need to be made have to be funded.

In my experience, once a management team is satisfied with the above points, they are likely to agree to a pilot of ONEplus therapy rather than the unpiloted complete introduction of this form of therapy delivery (see the section on 'Piloting ONEplus Therapy' below).

Therapists

As the agency's therapists will be the ones who deliver ONEplus therapy, they must be committed to its introduction. For therapists to give this commitment, they first need to understand what ONEplus therapy is and what it isn't, and they then need to be trained in its application within the agency. In my view, these two areas should be dealt with separately.

A half-day introduction to ONEplus therapy

First, there should be a half-day presentation by someone knowledgeable and skilled in ONEplus therapy which outlines the nature of ONEplus therapy, the theory that underpins it and its central practical tenets. At this meeting, it is vital that therapists have an opportunity to ask questions about ONEplus therapy and voice any doubts, reservations and objections (DROs) to this form of therapy delivery. The role of the trainer here is critical. The trainer must respond to all questions and DROs with respect and clarity. The trainer's goal here is to give everybody at the workshop an opportunity to ask questions and share their concerns about ONEplus therapy so that they can go away with an accurate understanding of this form of therapy delivery.

Ideally, after the half-day workshop, there should be a meeting where therapists can discuss what they took from the workshop and decide if they wish to practise ONEplus therapy if the agency chooses to integrate it into its therapeutic offerings. In the same way that no client should be forced to have ONEplus therapy, no therapist should be compelled to practise it if they do not wish to.

Training in ONEplus therapy

In Chapters 2 and 3, I outlined the knowledge and general skills that ONEplus therapists need to develop in a training course. However, I know that most people who wish to practise ONEplus therapy in an agency setting will not want to do a Certificate-level course in ONEplus therapy that lasts 24 hours. However, there should be minimum training standards that need to be met before a person should practise ONEplus therapy. These standards can be met in a two-day training programme lasting 12 hours. Agency-based training should include the following:[28]

- The nature of ONEplus therapy.
- The assumptions of ONEplus therapy.
- The ONEplus therapy mindset (compared to the conventional therapy mindset).
- An overview of the practice of ONEplus therapy.
- Helping clients prepare for ONEplus therapy.
- Contracting with and engaging clients in ONEplus therapy.
- Beginning ONEplus therapy.
- Facilitating change in ONEplus therapy.
- Ending ONEplus therapy.
- Getting feedback and following up.

In addition, participants should watch the trainer conduct at least one demonstration of ONEplus therapy and preferably two with members of the agency's therapy team seeking help with a genuine, current issue that they do not mind discussing in front of a group of their colleagues.

After watching the demonstration(s), therapists should pair up and have the private opportunity of helping the other person with a genuine issue in a ONEplus therapy context. Within the pair, there should be two full sessions so that both can be therapist and client. After the sessions, the whole group reconvenes, and therapists can share their experiences of the exercise. This peer counselling is a non-negotiable part of the two-day training course.

As in the half-day introductory workshop, throughout the two-day training, therapists should be encouraged to ask

---

[28] I cover all of these issues in this book.

questions and raise doubts, reservations and objections (DROs) with the trainer, who, as before, should respond with respect and clarity.

Funders

Funders must provide financial resources for a pilot study into how ONEplus therapy works in the agency so that a decision can be made to introduce this form of therapy delivery into the agency. If they do not, ONEplus therapy will not get off the ground. Even if the funders agree to underwrite the pilot financially, they should be prepared to provide the financial resources for fully integrating ONEplus therapy into the agency, should the pilot study prove successful. This may mean providing extra funds for additional therapists and/or additional administrative staff.

The pilot study should not occur unless the latter undertaking is given. I say this because if the pilot study is successful, but the funders will not resource the integration of ONEplus therapy into the agency, then the pilot study is a waste of time and money. Also, failure to proceed with such integration when a pilot has been successful will have a negative impact on staff who favour the introduction of ONEplus therapy into the agency and who have worked hard to try to make it happen.

Administrators

I believe administrators should take part in the initial half-day introduction to ONEplus therapy to understand what it is and what it has to offer the agency's clientele. After this, administrators have a crucial role in shaping how ONEplus therapy can be best integrated into the agency from an administrative point of view.

Clients

It is common for agencies to seek feedback on their services from users of that service.[29] Indeed, the UK's National Health Service has a legal duty to involve service users when planning and developing services.[30] Before implementing the pilot study mentioned above, I suggest the agency consults potential clients of ONEplus therapy to get their views on this therapy delivery and how it might best meet their therapeutic needs. Then after the pilot has been completed, a group of clients that have used the ONEplus therapy service can be convened to give their feedback on their experiences of the service. Their feedback should influence how ONEplus therapy will eventually be integrated into the agency's services.

The Importance of Training, Supervision, Research and CPD

Once ONEplus therapy has been introduced into an agency, several activities need to be put in place to ensure that it thrives in the agency. These are:

Training

For new agency therapists to work in the ONEplus therapy service, they need to be trained to do so. Thus, the agency needs to think about how it will train new therapists to get training equivalent to that given to those who attended the two-day training described above.

Supervision

Ongoing supervision of ONEplus therapy work, at least monthly, needs to be carried out by a supervisor experienced in the practice of ONEplus therapy and its supervision. Some agencies think that

---

[29] Known as 'service users'.
[30] This is known as 'Patient and Public Involvement (PPI)'.

ONEplus therapy can be supervised by someone skilled in conventional therapy supervision, but, in my view, this is erroneous (see Chapter 4).

Research

Data from agencies that have introduced ONEplus therapy have found that in 50% of cases, the client is happy with a single session and requests no further help. The agency in question, which has just incorporated ONEplus therapy into its therapy delivery offerings, needs to collect data to determine whether a similar pattern occurs after its introduction.

In addition, pre- and post-measures of client functioning should be completed by clients as this is the only *objective* way of determining the helpfulness of ONEplus therapy. In addition, a sample of ONEplus therapy clients should be interviewed to get their *subjective* experiences of this way of working with clients. See Chapter 11 for material on the use of follow-up in ONEplus therapy.

Continuing professional development

Assuming that the agency has decided to integrate ONEplus therapy into its overall service provision, then thought needs to be given to the continuing professional development of participating therapists. There are two approaches to this. First, each therapist is invited to nominate a few CPD events they would like to attend based on their experiences working as a ONEplus therapist in the agency. Second, the therapist team comes together and nominates a few CPD events that they would like to attend as a team. These should be included in the agency's overall budget for running ONEplus therapy.

Piloting ONEplus therapy

For a pilot to take place, therapists in the agency interested in being a part of the pilot should be identified and trained to do the work. Once they have received adequate training (see Chapters 2 and 3), their actual work needs to be supervised by a ONEplus therapy supervisor (see Chapter 4).

For a successful pilot, the following conditions should be met:

- The agency must recruit clients for the pilot via their website and other means. ONEplus therapy should be accurately described, and what a pilot is should also be made clear.

- No attempt should be made to assess the client's suitability for ONEplus therapy. The client's decision to seek it should be sufficient.

- An agreed number of therapists should be recruited for the pilot, each seeing a set number of clients over the pilot's life. In my view, if there are five therapists, each should see twenty clients; if there are ten therapists, each should see ten clients.

- To ensure that the 'help at the point of need' nature of ONEplus therapy is preserved, clients should be seen within a week of first approaching the agency for help.

- Once the client has made an appointment, their assigned therapist should email them to introduce themself to the client and send them a pre-session questionnaire designed to help them to prepare for the session so that they can get the most from the session. The therapist should stress that completing the form is recommended, not mandatory. If the client completes the form, they should be invited to send a copy back to the therapist, who can prepare themselves for the session (see Chapter 7).

- Ideally, the agency should offer clients who want more help a choice of therapy services offered.

- The agency must decide which objective measures to use to determine how clients respond to ONEplus therapy and when to complete these pre- and post-ONEplus therapy. In addition, qualitative data should be collected from some clients to discover their experiences of having ONEplus therapy.

- A report should be written based on the findings of the study together with feedback from service users. Then, a final decision should be made concerning whether or not to formally introduce ONEplus therapy as a form of therapy delivery alongside the agency's other clinical offerings. If so, and assuming that this will be appropriately funded, plans to integrate this service should involve all therapists wishing to be a part of the ONEplus therapy delivery and those involved in the service's administration.

In Part III of this book, I will focus on the practice of ONEplus therapy.

Part III

The Practice of ONEplus Therapy

PREAMBLE

In this part of the book, I will focus on the practice of ONEplus therapy, whether in independent practice or within a therapy agency. I will begin in Chapter 7 with how to help clients prepare for their participation in ONEplus therapy. Then, in Chapter 8, I will focus on how to get ONEplus therapy off on the best foot. In Chapter 9, I will turn my attention to the issue of how to facilitate change in ONEplus therapy. Given that most clients seek ONEplus therapy for help with finding a solution to a specific emotional or behavioural problem with which they are stuck, I will work on the assumption that this type of help is what your client has come for. In Chapter 10, I will discuss how to end well in ONEplus therapy and will pay particular attention to presenting different future options in an even-handed way. In Chapter 11, I will discuss the issues of getting immediate client feedback and following them up after some time. Finally, in Chapter 12, I present how I tend to practice ONEplus therapy. Please bear in mind that when I do so, I am *not* suggesting that you practise ONEplus therapy as I do. Your task is to find a way of practising ONEplus therapy that suits you and benefits your clients.

7

Helping Your Client to Prepare for the Session

There is a minority view in the single-session community that SST should be one session and no more – no pre-session contact or follow-up. However, most people think that this is too limiting. Indeed, in ONEplus therapy, pre-session contact and follow-up are routine parts of this therapy delivery. In this chapter, I will discuss how you can help your client prepare for the first and perhaps only session they will have in ONEplus therapy. Such preparation encourages your client to get the most from the session.

Once a person makes a ONEplus therapy appointment, the assigned therapist writes to the person to introduce themself and to request that the person completes a pre-session form. One of the reasons that the therapist does this is to make effective use of the time between the person making an appointment for ONEplus therapy and the session taking place. Appendix 5 contains an example of such a communication.

Pre-Pandemic vs Post-Pandemic

Before the pandemic, in my independent practice, I distinguished between having a telephone conversation (lasting for approximately 30 minutes) designed to help the client prepare for their session with me and the session itself, which would take place face-to-face. The preparation phone call would occur one or two days after the person first made contact,[31] and the face-to-face session would occur two or three days after that. During the pandemic, most therapeutic services took place via online platforms (e.g., Zoom). Given this, and because I felt it necessary to distinguish between preparing for the session and the session itself, I decided to make the following changes. First, instead of having a telephone preparation session with a client, I sent them a pre-session questionnaire to complete and return.[32] Then, two or three days later, we would have the session via Zoom. In truth, I have not found a significant difference from a therapeutic perspective in conducting ONEplus therapy face-to-face or by Zoom. The latter is more convenient for clients who are spared the time and expense of travelling to my office in the West End of London.

Preparation by Telephone or by Questionnaire

The main difference between helping clients prepare by telephone and by questionnaire is that the former is often more productive because it is interactive. I can ask follow-up questions if necessary. However, the latter gives the person more time to reflect, given that I am not at the other end of the telephone line, and they can complete the questionnaire at their leisure, in several sittings if they wish. In my experience, in about 15% of cases where I have conducted a pre-session preparation session by telephone, the person found this conversation sufficient and did not require a face-to-face session. This only very rarely happens with the pre-session questionnaire. It is the interactive nature of the telephone conversation, where I ask follow-up questions if need be, that more closely approximates a ONEplus therapy session than does the client completing the questionnaire

---

[31] See Appendix 6 for my pre-session telephone protocol. The spaces to the right are for the notes I took from the conversation.

[32] See Appendix 7 for my pre-session questionnaire. The document is in Word and the boxes expands according to how much the client writes.

on their own. As such, the telephone conversation has greater therapeutic potency for clients completing the questionnaire.

On the other hand, from a cost and time expenditure point of view, completing the questionnaire has advantages for the client and the agency. From the client's perspective, completing the questionnaire is much cheaper for them than having a 30-minute telephone conversation with an independent practitioner. The costs of the latter are appreciably greater than those of the former. From the agency's perspective, there is a greater time expended when an agency therapist conducts a 30-minute conversation than when they process the client's questionnaire responses. Thus, it is much more likely that agencies will choose to use the 'preparation by questionnaire' method than the 'preparation by telephone' method.

*

I have presented my telephone protocol in Appendix 6 and my pre-session questionnaire in Appendix 7. I have included them in this book as examples of how *one* ONEplus therapist has approached the task of preparing clients for ONEplus therapy. This should not be taken as me stating how *all* ONEplus therapists should carry out such preparation. Each ONEplus therapist in independent practice and each therapy agency should design their own forms for their own purposes.

8

Beginning the Session Well

Getting ONEplus therapy off to a good start is paramount, and there are several ways of doing this, as I will discuss in this chapter.

Ensuring Informed Consent

Like other ways of working with clients, the ethical practice of ONEplus therapy is based on the client giving informed consent to proceed.[33] As the term makes clear, informed consent has two components. The client needs to be informed about the nature of ONEplus therapy, and once this has been done, they need to consent to proceed. Even if the client has read about ONEplus therapy on the website of an agency or an independent practitioner, the therapist still needs to clarify that the client understands its nature.

Therapist: Before we start, what do you understand about what we will do today?

Client: Well, I was told that we would have one therapy session, and that is it.

---

[33] Gaining a client's informed consent is one aspect of contracting. Other issues, including agreeing on confidentiality and other practical issues, are done in ONEplus therapy. Still, as they are common to all forms of therapy delivery, I won't discuss them here.

Therapist:	That is not the case. I will endeavour to help you today with whatever you wish to discuss with me, but that more help is available for you in the future if you think you need it.
Client:	So, I'm not restricted to one session?
Therapist:	Not at all. You may not need more than one session, but you are not restricted to one session.
Client:	That sounds better.
Therapist:	So, would you like to proceed on that basis?
Client:	Yes, I would

Beginning ONEplus Therapy If There Has Been Pre-Session Preparation

As I have previously noted, a small group of therapists hold that ONEplus therapy should be a single session with no preparation or follow-up. However, most believe these latter activities should be a part of ONEplus therapy. When clients are invited to prepare for the session by completing a pre-session questionnaire (see Chapter 7), this should be considered when beginning the session.

Therapist:	Thank you for completing the pre-session questionnaire.
Client:	You're welcome.
Therapist:	Can I refer to the questionnaire, if necessary, in the session?

Client: Yes, of course.

Therapist: Thanks. Now, what changes, if any, have you noticed between completing the questionnaire and the session today?

The therapist proceeds according to the client's response to this question. If the client has noticed any changes, then the therapist would begin with this and help them both understand what occasioned the change and how this could be capitalised upon. On the other hand, if the client has not noticed any changes, the therapist would ask a question from one of the following sections.

In these sections, I will assume that the client has not done any pre-session preparation.

Beginning ONEplus Therapy by Focusing on Its Purpose

As I have noted, several therapy agencies seek to introduce ONEplus therapy in order to reduce their waiting lists. However, while ONEplus therapy services have this *effect,* their *intent* is, as has already been discussed, to provide help at the point of need and to see if therapists can help clients achieve their therapeutic goals in a single session, knowing that more help can be accessed if needed. Given that ONEplus therapy has a purpose, this is reflected in the following opening question.

Therapist: From your perspective, what is the purpose of our conversation today?

Asking this question enables the therapist to discover quickly if the client has a realistic view of the purpose of ONEplus therapy or not. If not, the therapist can be clear about what they can and can't do, helping orient the client to the therapeutic potency of this form of therapy delivery.

Beginning ONEplus Therapy by Asking about the Client's Problem

As most clients seek ONEplus therapy for help with a problem, another common way of beginning SST is for the therapist to be problem-focused.[34] For example:

Therapist:	What problem, concern or issue would you like to discuss with me?
	or
Therapist:	What problem, concern or issue would you like me to help you with?

Beginning ONEplus Therapy by Asking about the Client's Goals

In my view, when a person seeks help with a problem, they have a goal in mind – although they may need assistance to express this – and the therapist needs to help the client to identify a solution that effectively addresses the problem and helps them to achieve their goal. The goal-directed nature of SST is reflected in the following beginning questions.

---

[34] A therapist who practises ONEplus therapy from a solution-focused perspective might decide *not* to ask a problem-focused question as they would want to be solution-focused in their questioning.

Therapist: What would you like to achieve by talking with me today?

or

Therapist: What would you like to take away from our conversation that would make it worthwhile that you came today?

As I have previously mentioned, I distinguish in ONEplus therapy between a goal related to the client's nominated problem and a goal related to what the client wants to achieve by the end of the session. If the client mentions the former, the therapist can usefully ask about the latter and help them see that achieving their session goal can be a prelude to achieving their problem-related goal.

Beginning ONEplus Therapy by Asking about What Help the Client Is Seeking

While most clients seem to want help to solve an emotional problem in ONEplus therapy, other forms of help are available. A different way of beginning ONEplus therapy is to ask about the type of help the client seeks from the therapist.

Therapist: How can I be most helpful to you today?

or

Therapist: What help would you like from me today?

If the client initially struggles to answer the question, the therapist should give them alternatives, as shown below.

Therapist:	What help would you like from me today?
Client:	I'm not sure.
Therapist:	Well, there are several ways in which I could be helpful. Can I summarise them, and you can tell me which one resonates most with what you think would be most helpful?
Client:	That would be useful.
Therapist:	Well. I could help you to develop a greater understanding of an issue; I could just listen while you talk about an issue; I could help you to express your feelings about an issue; I could help you to solve an emotional or behavioural problem with which you feel stuck; I could help you to make a decision if that were relevant, or I could help you resolve a dilemma. Do any of these describe the kind of help you are looking for?

Sometimes a client may ask for a form of help that the therapist may be reluctant to give. In this case, it is vital that the therapist is transparent about what they are prepared to do and what they are not prepared to do, as in the following.

Therapist:	How can I be most helpful to you today?
Client:	I would like you to advise me on which job offer to take.
Therapist:	Well, therapy is very different from advice-giving. So, I won't do that. However, I would be more than happy to look at the options that you have with you and help you to figure out which course of action to take based on what's important to you rather than on what I think you should do. How does that sound?
Client:	That sounds OK.

Beginning ONEplus Therapy: The Gloria Films

As I discussed in Chapter 1, perhaps the most famous films in the history of psychotherapy have come to be known as the 'Gloria Films'. In these films, 'Gloria' (not her real name) had what can be seen now as a single, 'one-off' session of therapy with each of three well-known therapists: Carl Rogers (the developer of what is now known as Person Centred Therapy), Fritz Perls (the developer of Gestalt Therapy) and Albert Ellis (the developer of what is now known as Rational Emotive Behaviour Therapy or REBT). Each session lasted 30 minutes or less. For the present purposes, I will reflect on how each therapist began their session with 'Gloria'. As will be seen, each opening gambit reflects, to some degree, the central ideas of the approach to therapy that is being demonstrated. This shows that the therapist's assumptions underpin even simple beginning questions.

Carl Rogers: Now then, we have half an hour together, and I really don't know what we will be able to make of it, but I hope we can make something of it. I'd be glad to know whatever concerns you.

Here, Rogers is tentative, hopeful and invitational in his beginning statement to Gloria, reflecting the person-centred approach. However, the phrase 'whatever concerns you' directs Gloria to her concerns and is thus somewhat inconsistent with the approach. A less directive phrase here would have been, 'I'd be happy to know whatever you choose to tell me.'

Fritz Perls: We are going to have an interview for half an hour.

Here, Perls is being mercurial, descriptive and in the 'here and now' in the way he begins the session. This is consistent with Gestalt Therapy principles and Perls' practice of them.

Albert Ellis: Well, would you like to tell me what's bothering you most?

Here, Ellis is consistent with the problem-focused nature of REBT, although inconsistent with the ABC model propounded by the approach.[35] His statement implies a causality (something at A bothers the client at C) which is at variance with the model. A more accurate beginning would have been, 'Well, would you like to tell me what you are bothered about most?' Here, 'C' is deemed to be about 'A' and not caused by it.

Helping the Client to Create a Focus for the Session

Once you have initiated ONEplus therapy, your next task is to help the client identify a focus for the session. You can ask several questions to help the client create a focus. These questions can be problem-oriented, solution-focused or goal-focused. In ONEplus therapy, a solution helps the person address their problem effectively so that they can achieve their goal. You may have already asked one or more of these questions initially, but now is the time to ask them if you still need to.

---

[35] Here, 'A' stands for adversity, 'B' stands for the person's basic attitude towards the adversity and 'C' stands for the emotional and behavioural consequences of the basic attitude.

Questions that Help Create a Problem Focus for the Session

If you think it is best to have a problem focus for the session, you can ask the following questions:

Therapist: What problem do you want to focus on today?

or

Therapist: What one issue can I help you focus on today?

If the client comes up with more than one, you need to help them to choose the one they want to start with, and if there is time, you can help them with the other one.

Questions that Help Create a Solution Focus for the Session

If you think it is best to have a solution focus for the session, you can ask the following questions:

Therapist: If I could help you today to find a way of addressing your problem effectively, would you be interested in focusing on that?

or

Therapist: If I could help you to find a solution to your problem today that you could take forward to achieve your goal, would you be interested in that as a focus for today?

Questions that Help Create a Goal Focus for the Session

If you think it is best to have a goal focus for the session, you can ask the following questions:

Therapist:	Would a useful focus be for us to discover what you would like to achieve by the end of the session and work towards that end?

or

Therapist:	When you are at home this evening and reflect on our session today, what would you have liked to have achieved? [*After the client provides the answer.*] Would us working together to help you to achieve that be a good focus for today?

After the therapist has asked the client a focus-oriented question, the client's response will either indicate that a focus can be created from that response or that the therapist needs to ask further clarificatory questions. It is also important to note that the therapist may begin by asking about a problem focus and then, depending on the client's response, use that to agree on a solution or a goal focus. This also occurs in the following exchange.

Therapist:	What one issue can I help you with today?
Client:	I have been quite anxious lately.
Therapist:	Anxious about what?
Client:	Anxious about my son not getting into the school of his choice.
Therapist:	What effect does your anxiety have on you?

Client:	I have sleepless nights and can't concentrate on my work.
Therapist:	How do you hope I can help you with this problem today?
Client:	Help me to get some sleep and help me to concentrate on my work.
Therapist:	So, if I can help you address your anxiety about your son's schooling so that you can sleep and concentrate on your work, what would you think of that?
Client:	That would be great.
Therapist:	So, shall we agree that this will be the focus of the session
Client:	Yes.

Helping the Client to Maintain the Agreed Focus

Once you and your client have agreed on a focus, you must both maintain this focus if you are going to use session time well. It is your primary task to ensure that this focus is maintained. You can use a variety of skills to do this.

Seeking and Gaining Permission to Interrupt the Client

When I received training as a therapist almost 50 years ago, interrupting the client was strictly forbidden. The therapist's primary task was to encourage the client to explore their concerns and to follow them in their exploration rather than to guide them in any direction. Therefore, there was no reason to interrupt the client. Apart from that, interrupting the client was seen as being rude. In ONEplus therapy, interrupting is regarded very differently. Once a session focus has been agreed upon, you need to maintain it during the session. As interrupting the client *may* be seen by the latter as being rude, I recommend that you first provide the client with a rationale for interrupting them and then seek their permission to do so. Here is an example:

Therapist:	Now that we have agreed on a focus for the session, we both need to maintain this focus. OK?
Client:	OK.
Therapist:	In any conversation between two people, it is easy for one or both to go from topic to topic, and in a social conversation, that is perfectly fine, but in a therapeutic conversation, when we have agreed on a focus, that is problematic. So, if that happens with us, I would like to interrupt you to bring us back to the focus. I will strive to do that as sensitively as possible, but I will need to do this. Do I have your permission to do so?
Client:	Yes, that is fine. I do tend to meander around sometimes.
Therapist:	How can I best interrupt you?
Client:	Just say, 'I'd like to interrupt you'.
Therapist:	OK, and feel free to interrupt me if I go off topic too.
Client: (laughing) I will.	

Checking that Both Are Maintaining the Focus

Sometimes it is difficult for you to know whether or not a client has wandered away from an agreed focus. Thus, at first sight, what appears to be a departure from the focus may be a necessary elaboration on a topic that clarifies the focus. Mutual dialogue is a critical feature in ONEplus therapy, so when this happens, check with the client that the focus is being maintained.

Therapist: Can I just something check with you?

Client: OK.

Therapist: We agreed to focus on your anxiety about your son's schooling, and I am aware that we are now discussing your wife spending a lot of time with her sister. I am unsure how this fits your anxiety about your son's schooling.

Client: It doesn't. I was going off track.

Therapist: So, shall we get back to your feelings of anxiety about your son not getting into his preferred school?

Client: Yes.

In the exchange above, the client acknowledges that they had gone off track. The following is an example where what is a departure from the focus actually clarifies the focus.

Therapist: Can I just something check with you?

Client: OK.

Therapist: We agreed to focus on your anxiety about your son's schooling, and I am aware that we are now discussing your daughter's problems at ballet school. I am not sure how that fits with your anxiety about your son's schooling.

Client:	The way I see it, they are both instances of my anxiety that my children may be blocked from getting what they want in life.
Therapist:	OK, I get that. They are linked. Would it make sense for us to maintain the focus on your son and then see if we can generalise to the situation with your daughter?
Client:	If we could do both today, that would be great.
Therapist:	OK, let's do that.

In this latter exchange, the client's seeming departure from the agreed focus (anxiety about the client's son's schooling) turned out to be a clarification of the focus (anxiety about the client's children not getting what they want in life). The former is a specific example of the latter, and the client's introduction of his daughter was another example of the broader focus. Note how the therapist acknowledged the link and suggested they remain with the specific instance of the now broadened focus (anxiety about the client's son's schooling). The therapist then indicated that the client could generalise any learning to the other particular instance of the broadened focus (anxiety about the client's daughter's difficulties at ballet school).

This latter example shows how you can work with both the specific and the general in ONEplus therapy, ensuring that both types of issues are connected.

Once you and your client have co-created a focus for the session and have an agreed way of maintaining this focus, the stage has been set for you to facilitate change for the client, which is the next chapter's topic.

9

Facilitating Change in the Session

In Chapter 2, I noted that people come to ONEplus therapy for different types of help. However, as the most frequent type of help that they seek is to address effectively a particular emotional or behavioural problem with which they are stuck, I will concentrate on this type of help in this chapter.

Also, in Chapter 2, I presented the following diagram, which I will use as a framework for this chapter.

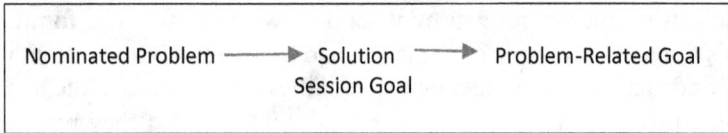

Nominated Problem ⟶ Solution ⟶ Problem-Related Goal
Session Goal

This shows:

- The problem that you and your client have agreed to focus on in the session. I call this the nominated problem, as the client may have other problems that are not the session's focus.

- The client has in mind a goal that relates to this problem which, if achieved, renders the problem non-problematic. For example, to feel un-anxiously concerned about criticism rather than to feel anxious about criticism. It is unlikely that the client will achieve their problem-related goal in the session. However, it does provide a direction after the session ends.

The solution addresses the person's problem and, if acted upon, helps the person reach their problem-related goal. In our example, it enables the client to feel un-anxiously concerned about criticism. Quite often, the solution is often what is known in ONEplus therapy as the session goal. This is what the person wants to achieve by the end of the session. As mentioned earlier in this book, a person often wants to take away some tips and techniques. These can best be seen as possible solutions that, if the person implements, can help them achieve their problem-related goal.

Factors Relevant to the Co-Construction of a Solution

In this chapter, I will discuss several factors that are relevant to the co-construction of a solution, which, if implemented, will facilitate change for the client. Regard these as a handy person would the tools they have in their toolbox. They won't need to use all the tools, but they are there if needed.

Understand the Nominated Problem in Context

In my view, it is important that you understand your client's nominated problem from their perspective.[36] Then you need to assess the problem using the constructs you tend to bring to therapeutic work. Here, different therapists will bring different constructs to the work. It is also helpful to understand the problem in context. This is particularly important when the person is seeking help for interpersonal problems. Understanding the history of these relationships can be helpful, as long as you do not spend too much time on this.

---

[36] Solution-focused, ONEplus therapists may not focus on the problem.

Understanding problem-maintaining factors

It is vital that you identify and help your client to understand the factors that serve to unwittingly maintain the problem. Often, the opposite of these factors can be integrated into the solution to the problem. Common problem-maintaining factors include:

- Avoidance factors
- Safety-seeking behaviour while remaining in the problem situation
- Lack of social support
- Meta-emotional problems (having an emotional problem about one's nominated problem)
- Compensatory behaviours
- Negative thinking
- Distress intolerance
- Discomfort intolerance
- Substance misuse

Working with a specific example

In assessing your client's nominated problem, it is useful to ask them to identify a specific example of this problem. This may be a recent example of the problem, a typical example of the problem or a predicted example of the problem. Being specific allows the client to more easily identify the factors that must be considered when devising a workable solution to the problem. The reason I favour working with a predicted example of the nominated problem is that the situation in which the problem has been assessed is the same as the situation in which the person plans to implement the solution.

Previous Helping Experiences

Your client will likely have made previous attempts to seek help before coming to see you. This may have been from friends, relatives or other helping professionals. If so, it is important that you discover what they found helpful and unhelpful in doing so. Your task is to encourage them to incorporate the helpful strategies into the solution they will construct and cast aside the unhelpful strategies.

Previous Self-Helping Experiences

In addition, your client has probably made a number of attempts to help themself deal with the problem for which they are seeking your help. If so, it is again important that you discover what they have found productive in terms of self-help and what wasn't useful for them. As before, your task is to help them to incorporate the helpful strategies into the solution they will construct and cast aside the unhelpful strategies.

Previous Success Experiences of Solving the Problem

It may be the case that your client has had a previous successful experience solving the very problem for which they are seeking help. For example, when a client says that they can't do something that they want to do because they don't have the confidence to do it, I proceed as follows:

Windy:	So, from your perspective, you can't apply for the job you want because you don't have the confidence to do it, is that right?
Client:	That's right.
Windy:	Have you ever had the experience where you did something you wanted to do, but initially you thought you did not have the confidence to do it?
Client:	Yes, I have.

Windy:	Tell me about it.
Client:	Well, I wanted to learn to drive, but at the beginning, I wasn't confident that I could do it.
Windy:	So, what did you do?
Client:	I decided to learn to drive even though I lacked confidence.
Windy:	And what happened?
Client:	I learned to drive.
Windy:	And when did you become confident driving?
Client:	After I had driven for a while.
Windy:	So, you wanted to drive, you lacked the confidence to drive, you decided to learn to drive without confidence, and eventually, you became confident after driving for a while. Is that right?
Client:	Yes.
Windy:	What would happen if you took that process and applied it to your current problem?

Internal Strengths

ONEplus therapy can be appropriately considered a strengths-based approach to therapy in that the ONEplus therapist strives to discover the client's strengths which they can use in the creation, rehearsal and implementation of the solution the client is seeking to address their nominated problem.

You can ask your client directly for their strengths. For example:

Therapist:	What strengths do you have as a person that you can use to help yourself address your problem?

Or you can ask for these strengths more indirectly. For example:

Therapist: What strengths would your friends say that you had as a person that you could use to help yourself address your problem?

or

Therapist: Suppose you went for an interview for a job you really wanted. Imagine they asked you what your strengths were as a person. What would you say in response that would be directly relevant to you in helping yourself address your problem?

You can also discern a client's strengths in what they have been saying so far in the session. For example:

Therapist: From what you say, I'm impressed with your persistence at trying to solve the problem. Am I right?

Client: I guess so.

Therapist: Would people who know you think that persistence was a strength of yours?

Client: Yes.

Therapist: So, once we have found a better solution for you, do you think that your persistence will help you to implement it?

Client: Yes, I think so.

External Resources – Interpersonal and Organisational

There is a phrase that I often use in ONEplus therapy with clients who are wary of asking others for help. It is, 'Only you can do it, but you don't have to do it alone'. This indicates that the client is primarily responsible for addressing their problem, but others can contribute process. Here are several questions you can ask your client with respect to external resources. The first two questions refer to people who can be of service:

Therapist: Which people in your life can be helpful to you as you address this problem? What help can they give you?

or

Therapist: Who on your team can you contact for specific help with this issue? Who are they, and what help would you want from them?

The following two questions refer to organisations and the broader term 'external resources':

Therapist: Are there any organisations that you know of who can help provide some help with this? Which organisations are they, and what help can they provide? [*You can make suggestions if they cannot think of any*]

or

Therapist: What external resources can you use to address the problem? [*Again, you can make suggestions if relevant.*]

Role Models

While helping your client think about possible solutions to their problem, it might be useful to ask them to select a role model they think has the skills or qualities to employ a potential solution successfully. By this, I mean that the solution will address their nominated problem successfully and help them achieve their problem-related goal. First, ask your client to specify these skills and qualities and whether they can emulate them. If the person thinks they can, encourage them to imagine emulating the role model, but in their own way. If they can do so successfully, then this tends to increase the chance that they will select the potential solution as their chosen solution.

Here is an example of doing this in action.

Windy:	Can you think of someone in your life, past or present, who handles criticism in the way that you want to handle it?
Client:	Yes, my late grandfather.
Windy:	How would he handle criticism?
Client:	He would say he didn't take things personally when he was criticised. He said that if the person had a point, he would think about it, and if they didn't, he would dismiss it.
Windy:	And you would like to be able to deal with criticism like that?
Client:	Yes, I would.
Windy:	So, he mentioned two things: don't take criticism personally and only consider criticism if it is valid. How do you fare on both of these?
Client:	I really struggle with the 'don't take things personally' point.

Windy:	In what way?
Client:	To be honest, I've never understood what it means.
Windy:	And it isn't easy implementing something if you don't know what it means.
Client:	Definitely.
Windy:	Would you say you take things personally when you are criticised?
Client:	For sure.
Windy:	So, first, would it make sense for us to understand what happens when you take things personally? Then we can figure out together what not taking things personally means.
Client:	That would really help.

I then helped the client understand the processes involved when he took criticism personally. He was then clearer about what he needed to do in order not to take being criticised personally. In spelling out the latter, he could understand for the first time what his grandfather meant by the term. This helped him become confident that, with practice, he could use this as a good solution to help him become un-anxiously concerned rather than anxious about criticism.

Sharoff (2002: 115–116) has outlined several steps that the ONEplus therapist can use to help the person emulate a role model in the service of solving their problem:

1. **Identify the model.**

2. **Overcome resistance to being like the model**. The client may think a gap between themselves and their chosen role model is too big. If so, you can either find ways to reduce the gap or help them choose a role model they can emulate.

3. **Show similarities between the model and the patient.**
   Unless the client sees such similarities, then the power of
   the role model as a facilitator of change is diminished.

4. **Encourage curiosity about the model's outstanding
   skills and how they operate.**

5. **Identify the model's skills and how they operate.** As I
   showed in the above example, for a person to emulate a
   role model, they need to be clear about what they are
   emulating. Only when I helped the client understand what
   'not taking criticism personally' means could he use his
   grandfather as a role model for change.

6. **Form a contract with the patient to work on
   developing those skills.** Here, it is important to help the
   client understand the skills that need developing before a
   contract can be made.

7. **Educate the patient about how to perform the needed
   skills.**

The Client's View of a Good Solution

It is a significant feature of the ONEplus therapy mindset
discussed in Chapter 2 that the client leads the work. As such, it
is vital that you seek your client's view on what they consider a
good solution to their nominated problem. If you don't do that,
you implicitly communicate to the client that their view on this
important issue is not worth considering. That being said, if you
ask your client for their view on what is a good solution to their
problem, this does not mean that you have to accept this view
uncritically. Indeed, you may think that your client's proposed
solution may make their nominated problem worse, not better. If
so, it is vital that you are clear about your reasoning on this point.
Otherwise, it is important that you utilise your client's views on
this point when formulating a solution with them.

The Therapist's View of a Good Solution

It is important for you as a ONEplus therapist to share your expertise on request without adopting the role of the expert. This means you ask your client if they are interested in your 'take' on a possible solution to their problem. When you offer your perspective on this point, it is important to stress that this is your viewpoint and not the only one on offer and that other therapists may have different views on the matter. Inform the client that they can draw upon your proposed solution or disregard it as they see fit.

Potential Solutions

ONEplus therapy does not prioritise one set of solutions over others. Remember that ONEplus therapy is client-led, so you will want to help your client select whichever solution they think is best for them, not which solution you think is best for them. There are a variety of solutions that clients can take from ONEplus therapy. I have categorised them as follows.

Reframing Solution

A reframe-based solution helps the person put a troublesome event into a new frame with the result that the problem is rendered non-problematic and can even be seen positively. The following story demonstrates this.

> An older woman had the habit of booking into a very exclusive hotel suite whenever she needed a few days' rest and quiet. When she did so, she made it very clear that she would require complete peace, free from all noise. As she lay on her bed, resting, she was awoken by loud piano music from the suite next door. Outraged, she went down to complain to the hotel manager. Skilled in handling delicate situations, the manager thought momentarily and then asked the woman if she had heard

of the man playing the piano in the suite next to hers. He told her that the pianist was an internationally renowned concert pianist in town for a single concert that had sold out months before. The woman confirmed that she had heard of the man. 'Madam,' said the hotel manager, 'do you know how fortunate you are? You are being given a private concert by one of the world's leading concert pianists!'. The woman's anger disappeared instantly, and she quickly excused herself, saying she did not want to miss any more of her private concert.

While not a ONEplus therapist, the hotel manager demonstrated all the hallmarks of one. He immediately focused on the woman's problem, thought quickly on his feet and reframed the problem from that which was an adversity for her (i.e., noise coming from next door which was disturbing her rest) to that which was an advantage for her (i.e., she was being given the opportunity of enjoying a private concert with a world-leading pianist).

Attitude Change Solution

An attitude is an evaluative stance that a person takes towards an adversity (Colman, 2015). When a person has a problem about an adversity, this is likely because the person holds a rigid and extreme attitude towards the adversity. The solution is helping the person develop an alternative flexible and non-extreme attitude towards the same adversity. Because this new attitude needs practising after the session, the main thing that you can do as a ONEplus therapist is to help the person to develop the attitude in the session, rehearse it to help the person get an experiential 'feel' of the new attitude and to help the person plan to put it into practice in the future.

Inference Change Solution

An inference is a person's hunch about reality, which may be correct or incorrect. Quite often, the client can never be sure about the validity of an inference and, therefore, can be encouraged to accept the 'best bet' about what happened, is happening or will happen. Here is an example where a client made an inference change when they could not make an attitude change.

> Here the therapist saw a middle-aged married woman who reported feeling furious every time her ageing father would telephone her and ask, 'Noo, what's doing?' She inferred that this was a gross invasion of her privacy and insisted that he had no right to do so (rigid attitude). The therapist initially intervened by encouraging the client to stand back and examine her rigid attitude that her father must not invade her privacy. All to no avail. Changing tack, he began implementing a different strategy designed to help the client question her inference that her father was invading her privacy. Given her father's age, the therapist inquired, was it not more likely that his question represented his usual manner of beginning telephone conversations rather than an intense desire to pry into her affairs? This enquiry proved successful in that the client's rage subsided because she began to reinterpret her father's motives.

Solution Based on a Change in the Person's Relationship with the Problem

Sometimes as a ONEplus therapist, you can help the person by facilitating a shift in their relationship to their problem. This may involve them seeing recognising what they saw as a dysfunctional response to an adversity was, in fact, quite an understandable one which many people would have made. This helps the person accept their response's existence rather than fight against it. Indeed, some ONEplus therapists who practise Acceptance and Commitment Therapy (ACT) argue that a person's struggle with troublesome emotions and thoughts is the problem. When the person stops struggling against these responses, they solve their problem (Bennett & Oliver, 2019).

Behavioural Change Solution

A solution based on a behaviour change is rooted in the idea that when a person changes their behaviour, they invite a different response from another person with whom they have a problem. Such a change on the part of your client does not guarantee that the other person will respond constructively, but it will increase the chances that this will happen.

In some areas, if your client takes action rather than choosing not to act, then they may improve the situation that they are in. For example, when a person chooses to do a task they have been putting off, it can positively impact their life.

In other areas, it is important that the person refrains from taking action rather than acting in self-defeating ways.

Situational Change Solution

Sometimes a person is best served if they change a situation that they are in. For example, a person may be working for a hyper-critical boss, and if no other solution will help the person, it is probably in their best interest to get a new job.

Change Based on a Combination of Solutions

While sometimes a person needs a single solution to their problem (e.g. reframing), they need a combination of solutions more frequently. For example, if a person needs to assert themself with someone, they not only need to change their behaviour but also their attitude in a way that supports assertion.

Rehearsing the Solution

Once your client has identified a solution that, in their view, is likely to work, then it is important that they have a chance to rehearse it in the situation if doing so is feasible. The purpose of this rehearsal is for your client to experience the solution in a controlled situation and to judge how it 'feels' for them to apply it. I liken this to the situation where before a person buys a new car, they take it for a test run to determine how it handles and if they feel comfortable driving it.

Methods of Solution Rehearsal

You may suggest various ways your client can rehearse the solution if it can be rehearsed. Here is a sample of such methods:

Chairwork

Chairwork involves the client addressing their problem while using chairs to facilitate dialogue between self and others or between different parts of self. As such, chairwork allows the client to rehearse their chosen solution where it involves such dialogue.

Role-play

Sometimes a client is uncomfortable using chairwork and may prefer to rehearse their selected solution in a role-play situation with you, as therapist, playing the role of the other person or that part of themself that the client needs to have a conversation with. When you play a role in the role-play, your client must brief you well so you can play the role accurately.

Imagery

When using imagery (or mental rehearsal) to rehearse a solution, it is important that the client sees themself enacting the solution in a coping capacity rather than masterfully. In the former case, they see themself initially implementing the solution with difficulty but persisting until they do it well. In the latter case, they see themself implementing the solution without any struggle. The former is realistic, while the latter is not.

If, after rehearsal, your client concludes that the solution 'feels' right, you can move to the action planning phase (see below). If the solution does not 'feel' right, you both need to determine whether the chosen solution can be 'tweaked' or if a new solution needs to be selected.

Developing an Action Plan

Once your client has decided on a solution after rehearsal, the next stage is for you to help them to develop an action plan so that the client can implement the solution. It should be noted that an action plan is different from a homework assignment. The latter is a specific task for the person to complete before the next session. The client and therapist then review the task at the beginning of the following session. When developing an action plan, it is important to remember that you may not see the person again. Thus, you will not be negotiating a specific task. Instead, you will be developing something broader with the client that has some or all of the following features:

- The solution to be implemented.
- Where the solution is to be implemented.
- When the solution is to be implemented.
- How often is the solution to be implemented.
- If the solution is to be implemented with other people, these people should be specified in the plan.

It is important to recognise that the more the client can integrate the action plan into their everyday life, the more likely it is that they will be able to implement it.

Identifying and Dealing with Potential Obstacles

After the action plan has been developed and guidelines for its implementation have been agreed upon, it is useful for you to encourage your client to consider what obstacles they may encounter in carrying out the plan. Once a potential obstacle has been identified, then your job is to help your client to find the best way to address the obstacle so that it does not, in fact, stop them from implementing it. Once you have done this, it is a good idea to suggest an imagery exercise, where your client encounters the obstacle mentioned above and sees themselves dealing with it constructively before picturing themself implementing the action plan.

Once you have helped your client to develop an action plan and aided them in dealing with any obstacles to implementing the plan, then this is a sign that you have approached the ending phase of the session, and you can begin the process of ending the session well which is the topic of the next chapter.

10

Ending the Session Well

Jerome Frank (1961) argued that while clients may come for therapy with a plethora of different symptoms, what unites them is that they come with a sense of demoralisation. The implication of this view for ONEplus therapy is that you need to help your client leave the session with their morale restored. This means that it is important that you end the session well. This involves you doing the following:

- Asking the client to summarise the session.
- Asking them what they are going to take away from the session.
- Exploring with your client whether they can generalise their learning to other issues they may have.
- Ensuring you tie up any loose ends with them.
- Being clear with them about their helping options.

Asking the Client to Summarise

After you have helped your client draw up an action plan and helped them identify and deal with any obstacles to implementing this plan, this ordinarily signals that the session is ending. Consequently, it is useful to ask the client to summarise the session. You might think it was more appropriate for you to summarise the session for the client, but this would not be in keeping with the ONEplus therapy mindset, which stresses the importance of the client's perspective. Your client's summary clarifies what they think you have both covered in the session. That is what they will be taking away. If, in your opinion, they have omitted something important, then you could mention it and see if they agree with you. Ideally, the client's summary should include their nominated problem, their chosen solution and their action plan.

Asking for the Client's Takeaways

If your client still needs to clarify what they will take away from the session, then you can ask them for this at this point. In addition to their selected solution, a takeaway should ideally include what the person has learned from the session that could make a difference in their life in the future.

Asking Clients to Generalise Their Learning to Other Issues

If feasible, it is a good idea to ask your client how they might generalise their learning to other issues that they may have. You need to take care when you do this. Otherwise, the client may take this as a cue to begin discussing other issues they may have. If this happens, you need to interrupt them and explain that your purpose is to help them see the possibilities of what they have learned rather than to do that work in the session with you.

Tying Up Loose Ends

It is important that the client does not have an 'I wish I'd mentioned that' or 'I wish I'd asked that' moment after the session. If they do, their post-session focus will be divided. Yes, they will focus on their takeaways and action plan, but they will also focus on what they did not say or ask. To minimise the chance of this happening, it is important that you ask your clients the following questions before the end of the session.

Therapist:	Do you wish to mention anything about the problem and what we discussed today that you wish you had mentioned when you think about the session later?
	and
Therapist:	Do you want to ask anything about the work we did today that you may have wished you had asked when you reflect on our session later on?

The goal of asking your client these questions is to give them a sense of completeness at the end of the session. However, it is crucial that you encourage your client to confine themself to the problem you discussed with them, the solution you co-created and their takeaways. The client should not take these two questions as an invitation to begin to talk about another matter at such a late stage. If they take it as such, you need to explain why they need to confine themself to what you discussed and not focus on what you did not discuss.

Reviewing Options for the Future

You will recall from Chapter 1 that I defined ONEplus therapy as follows:

'ONEplus therapy is an intentional form of therapy delivery where the therapist and client contract to meet for a session of therapy and work together to help the client to achieve their stated wants from that session on the understanding that further help is available to the client on request'.

Given that ONEplus therapy allows for the possibility that the client may seek additional help, it is important that you review your client's options with them at the end of the session.

My Approach

Let me begin with my approach to reviewing options for further help at the end of the session. I say something like this:

Windy: Before we close the session, let me outline possible ways forward. First, you may conclude that you have got what you came for from today's session and that you don't need any further help at this time. Second, you might like an opportunity to go away, reflect on the session, digest what you learned, put your action plan into practice and see what happens. At that point, you may decide you need no further help, or you may decide that you do. If so, please get back in touch with me. Third, you may decide that you would like further help, in which case, we can organise that now.

    I want you to know that each of these options is equally fine. The critical point is that you select the right option for you.

If the client asks for my opinion, I reiterate that the critical point is that they make their own decision on this point.

If the person selects the 'I want further help' option, I proceed as follows.

Windy: OK, well, here are the possibilities. In my practice, I can offer you another session, an agreed number of sessions decided by both of us or ongoing therapy. Also, if you want further help that I don't provide, I would be happy to refer you to someone who does provide that help. Which of these possibilities seems the right one for you?

Other Approaches

Agencies offering ONEplus therapy often inform the person that they will be called in two or three weeks to see how they are getting on and if they want further help. When this happens, the ONEplus therapy mindset suggests that the client is informed about what services the agency offers and the waiting time for each and then selects the service they wish to access.

At the very end of the session, after the person has decided how to proceed, arrangements are made for feedback and follow-up. I will discuss these topics in the next chapter.

Taking Notes in ONEplus Therapy

After the session is finished, it is customary for the ONEplus therapist to take notes on the session. The note-taking template that I use can be found in Appendix 8. I include it as *a* way of taking notes in ONEplus Therapy, not *the* way.

11

Getting Immediate Feedback and Following Up

In this chapter, I will consider getting immediate feedback from a client and then following up with a client.

Getting Immediate Feedback

Since you may not see your client again, it is helpful to understand what they made of their session with you. In my work for an online therapy agency where the modal number of sessions clients have is '1', I ask my clients at the end of these sessions if they would be prepared to complete a brief form so that I know how helpful the session was for them. Once they agree, I send them a form to complete and return (see Appendix 9).

Ideally, the client should send it back to someone other than the therapist since it is challenging to be critical if the client knows the therapist they have just seen will read the form.

This form can be handy for an agency offering ONEplus therapy as it will help them monitor the experiences of clients who see different therapists. This will help them to spot therapists who are not seen as helpful and thus prompt remedial action on behalf of the agency.

Following Up

The term 'follow up' is used in three ways in the single-session therapy community:

1. It is used when an agency or therapist contacts a client after the session to find out if they want more help. Some refer to this as 'following through'.

2. In a One-At-A-Time delivery service, when clients can only book one session at a time when the person returns after the first session, their next and subsequent sessions are known as follow-ups.

3. I use it to determine the longer-term effects of ONEplus therapy, whether the person has a single session or more. The discussion below is based on this usage of the term 'follow up'.

A few ONEplus therapists believe that in ONEplus therapy, the client should only have one contact (i.e., the therapy session) with the therapist and no more. From this perspective, there would be no follow-up.

However, most ONEplus therapists believe that this mode of therapy delivery does not preclude further help being available and believe that ONEplus therapy can be enhanced by both pre-session contact and follow-up. So, what are the reasons to follow up with clients who have had ONEplus therapy?

Why Follow Up?

Follow-up provides your client with an opportunity for feedback on what they have done between the single and follow-up sessions. In my experience, many clients appreciate such an opportunity.

Follow-up also provides you with outcome evaluation data (i.e. how the client has done).

These data can help you improve your delivery of ONEplus therapy.

Finally, follow-up provides the agency which offers ONEplus therapy with service evaluation data (the client's experience of seeking help from the agency). Such data can help the organisation improve its ONEplus therapy service.

When to Follow Up?

When a follow-up session is scheduled depends on whether ONEplus therapy takes place in a therapist's independent practice or an agency. If you work in independent practice, you and your client decide when to schedule the follow-up session. However, if you work in an agency, that decision will have been made by the agency's management.

My Approach to Follow Up

Here, I will discuss the situation where I conduct a longer-term follow-up with the client who has decided that they got what they wanted from their first and only session of ONEplus therapy.

My preference is to carry out the follow-up appointment by telephone. This is to make it distinct from the online ONEplus therapy session and have it interactive. For this reason, I prefer not to use a questionnaire for follow-up purposes. I have presented my follow-up telephone protocol in Appendix 10. Please note that I choose not to use objective forms to measure outcomes. I do realise, however, that many ONEplus therapists employ such measures, and if you do, you will need to give these to the client to complete pre-session and at follow-up.

*

In the final chapter, I will discuss my practice of ONEplus therapy.

Postscript

PREAMBLE

As you know by now, while there are some shared views of how to practise ONEplus therapy stemming from the ONEplus therapy mindset (see Chapter 2), no manual or protocol details how to practise this form of therapy delivery. Each therapist brings to the work ideas that inform their therapeutic work in general that they modify for use in ONEplus therapy. In Chapter 12, I will outline and discuss some ideas that inform my practice of ONEplus therapy. I am not suggesting, however, that you practise like me. I suggest, however, that you think about the ideas that inform your practice of ONEplus therapy. Before I share these ideas with you, I want to clarify that I do not impose them on a client. Instead, I ask them if they are interested in my take on the subject at hand, and when they say that they are, I present the idea in a way that indicates that this is only one way of looking at the topic and other perspectives may be equally valid.

12

Thirty Ideas that Inform My Practice of ONEplus Therapy

Here, then, in this final chapter, I present 30 ideas that inform my practice of ONEplus therapy. Remember, these are the ideas that inform *my* practice of ONEplus therapy, they are not ideas that should inform *your* practice of ONEplus therapy, and I am certainly not presenting them as ideas that should inform *the* practice of ONEplus therapy.

1. Making an Emotional Impact

In my view, it is important to strike a balance in ONEplus therapy between head and heart. Too much head and the client comes away from the session with some good theoretical ideas, but without the emotional resonance to promote change. Too much heart and the risk is that the client may have an emotionally cathartic experience but without any clear idea about what to apply from the session to their own life. In this respect, your goal as a ONEplus therapist is to create a therapeutic environment in which the session has a productive emotional impact on your client; productive in the sense that it both engages their heart and head which can work together to facilitate later change. Before I discuss how you can increase the session's emotional impact on the client, let me issue a caveat. You should not go into the session intent to provoke the client's emotions. Rather, take due care and look for ways to help the client connect their feelings with what they are discussing so that they can integrate their thoughts and emotions while searching for a solution.

Finding and Using Something that Really Resonates with Your Client While Helping Them

Knowing what will resonate with your client when you are helping them address their problem and/or search for a solution is difficult. I keep the following points in mind when I do this with my ONEplus therapy clients.

Using language that is meaningful to the client

I listen carefully to the language that the client uses in the session. If they use certain words or phrases frequently, then this may be one indication that such language is meaningful to them, particularly if it is accompanied by affect. Also, I may find that the client responds emotionally to certain words or phrases that they may use. In both cases, I endeavour to use such language with my client, but not overuse it. In the latter case, the client may think that I am being 'clever' or 'disingenuous', which are to be avoided, if possible.

Using relevant imagery

The same applies to any recurrent imagery which the client may use. Such imagery may indicate the client's preferred sensory modalities (e.g. visual, auditory, olfactory or sensory) and I encourage emotional engagement by talking the client's language when working with such imagery.

Utilise the visual medium as well as the verbal medium

ONEplus therapy is largely a talking therapy, and as such, there is a lot of verbal communication between myself and my client. However, to enhance the impact of SST, it is useful sometimes to present visual representations of verbal concepts, especially for those clients whose learning is enhanced by the visual medium. In Figure 1 (next page), I present the 'Big I-Little i' technique which shows that the 'Big I', which represents a person, is comprised of a myriad of aspects represented by little i's. It shows that a person cannot be defined by any of their parts. I use it to help the client to promote unconditional self-acceptance.

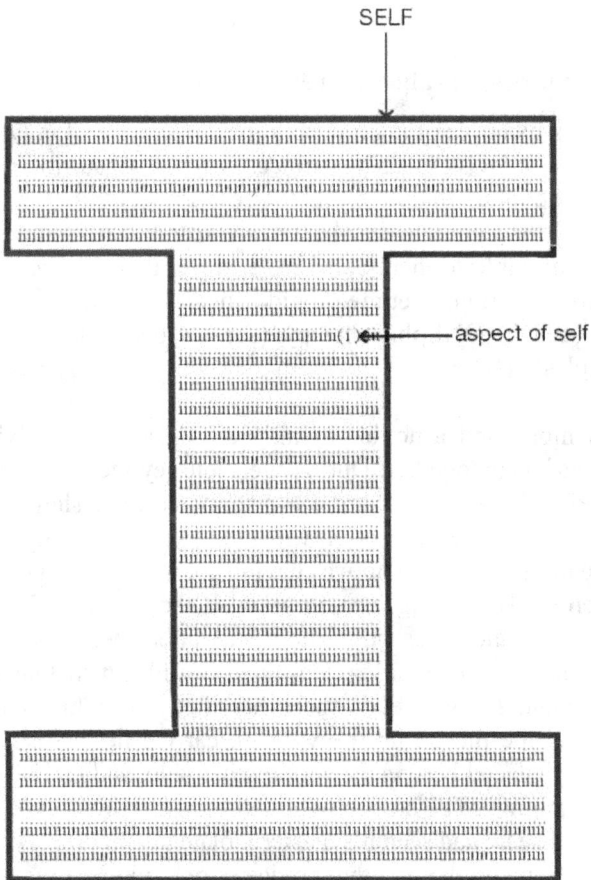

Figure 1 'The Big I – little i' technique

Refer to Your Client's Core Values to Promote Change

In my view, it is important for the ONEplus therapist to discover their client's core values during session. The purpose of this is so that the therapist can use these to help the client to connect their goals and goal-directed activities to their values. A client will probably strive more persistently towards a goal when it is underpinned by a core value than when it is not.

Using Stories, Parables and Metaphors

The final example of making an impact with a client in ONEplus therapy that I wish to discuss concerns the use of stories, parables and metaphors. I find it helpful to use a pertinent story or parable that presents a point to the client in a way that may be meaningful and memorable to them and is relevant to their problem and/or potential solutions. Let me provide one example of a story that I have used in ONEplus therapy (see Dryden, 2024) for other examples.

> A monk and a novice monk were on a silent walking pilgrimage together. During their journey they arrived at a river bank where there was a strong current. They were about to cross the river when they saw a young and beautiful woman who was having great difficulty getting across. The young woman asked if they could help her cross to the other side. The novice monk was horrified because in their order, they had vowed not to touch a woman. He was even more horrified when his senior colleague picked up the woman, carried her across the river, placed her gently on the other side, and carried on his journey. The novice was in turmoil as they walked on because he had seen his master violate an important vow. After many hours, the novice monk plucked up the courage and broke the silence. 'As monks, we have taken a vow not to touch a woman, how could you then pick up that young woman back at the river bank and carry her in

your arms?' The older monk looked at him and replied, 'My brother, I set her down on the other side of the river and have forgotten her because we have also taken a more important vow to help people in need, which I did. You, on the other hand, are still carrying the woman.

If it needs making, the point of this story is that sometimes you don't do the right thing because you are rigidly adhering to a principle and ignoring other important principles that need consideration. When you hold a rule rigidly and see someone break it, you spend hours ruminating on this. However, holding rules flexibly allows you to make healthy choices in the moment while recognising the complexity of life, even if it means breaking an important rule. You do so because it is more important to you to keep to another rule.

2. Using Humour

While ONEplus therapy is a serious business, it does not always have to be practised in a serious way. The use of humour in therapy has often been discussed and has its proponents and its critics (Lemma, 2000). One of its proponents was Albert Ellis, the founder of Rational Emotive Behaviour Therapy. Ellis (1977) argued that one way of viewing psychological problems was that it was the result of a person taking themself, others and/or life *too* seriously and that, consequently, the therapist could help the person by encouraging them to adopt a humorous perspective. They can best do this by using humour themself in the single session, if they have a sense of humour, which, sadly, not all therapists do, in my experience. In addition, the client may not have a sense of humour or, if they do, they might think that humour has no place in therapy. Given all this, the therapist needs to tread carefully when thinking about using humour in OnePlus therapy. However, taking due care, humour is an excellent way to help the client connect emotionally with what they have been saying in the session. It goes without saying that I try to have fun *with* the client rather than poke fun *at* my client.

Before using humour, I ask the client directly whether they think that humour has a place in therapy and whether they would value me offering a humorous perspective on their problem if I did so sensitively. If I do so, the impact of my humorous intervention is usually immediately apparent.

Swaminath (2006) has argued that the use of therapist humour can be of potential help to the client in the following ways:

- It creates a more relaxed atmosphere and helps break down barriers.
- It can convey the message that the therapist is humane.
- It can build trust and empathy if used appropriately.
- It can help the client to relax and talk more freely.
- It can convey messages succinctly and effectively.
- It encourages communication on sensitive matters.
- It can be a source of insight into conflict.

In addition, therapist humour can best help the client, in my view, by promoting constructive cognitive change within an emotionally aroused context (see Dryden, 2022b)

3. Utilising the 'User Manual' Approach

If you were to purchase a washing machine, it usually comes with a user manual which details what you need to do to get the most out of your appliance. The same concept can be utilised to help the client get the most from themselves and know how to interact with the people in their life so that they can deal with any relationship problems they may have with them. This helps the client respond to the other person based on what they know about how this person works rather than on how they think the other person should work.

4. Helping the Client to Respond to Their Initial Reactions

Some clients come to ONEplus therapy with the goal of not responding in their current problematic ways to the adversities that feature in their problems. This goal is unworkable because it goes against the ways humans function. As an alternative to the above, I have found it useful to offer a framework where the person accepts the reality that they probably will react initially in their usual problematic manner to the problem-based adversity. Still, they can respond healthily to this initial reaction. This involves the following process:

- Recognising the presence of the initial reaction.
- Accepting the existence of the reaction. Refrain from trying to eliminate it.
- Standing back to give oneself some distance to enable one to think about what to do next.
- Bringing to mind the alternative response to the adversity (i.e. their selected solution) and what one needs to do to implement this response.
- Recognising that implementing the new response is going to 'feel strange'.
- Implementing the new response.

Initially, executing the above steps will feel 'clunky'. However, the more the person does so, the more natural it will feel to the person.

The client needs to avoid the dangers of over-using their selected solution at any one time. Thus, they need to agree with themself that they will use their selected solution for a set, healthy period, after which they will disengage from it. I use the analogy of going to the gym to get fit. Well-spaced gym sessions, followed by rest are better than one massively long gym session.

5. Using the Book Analogy

Quite often, when a person nominates a problem to discuss in ONEplus therapy, the way they discuss it shows that when the problem occurs in a relevant situation, the client regards the beginning of the problem as the end of the story. The way I respond to this is rather than this being the end of the story; the client can view it as the end of Chapter 1 of a book. In Chapter 2, they have options for how they respond. I discuss these options with them, and they select one they think is the best solution to their problem. After they have tried this solution, Chapter 3 begins, and if needed, subsequent chapters culminate in the book's end, representing the client achieving their problem-related goal. I call this the 'book analogy'.

6. Helping the Client to Determine Whether They Have Solved the Problem Before

When a client seeks help for a problem from you as a ONEplus therapist, it is useful to remember that they may have solved the problem before but have not registered that they have done so. Given this possibility, it is worth asking the client about this. Here is an example:

Windy: So you want to discuss with me how to handle criticism in a constructive manner. Is that correct?

Client: That's correct.

Windy: Tell me about a time when you handled criticism well.

[*Note here that I assume that the person has handled criticism well and asked them to search for an example of this. If I had asked, 'Have you ever handled criticism well?' it would be easy for the person to reply in the negative.*]

Client: Yes, a few weeks ago, my colleague criticised me and it was so far off the mark that I just laughed it off.

Windy: So, you can handle criticism when it is obviously not true from your perspective.

Client: That's right. I hadn't thought of it like that before.

Windy: What if you think the criticism has some merit?

Client: That is when I struggle.

Windy: What's the difference from your perspective between criticism that is wrong and criticism that has some merit?

Client: I feel badly about myself when the criticism has some merit, and I don't feel badly about myself when it is wrong.

Windy: Tell me about a time when you did not feel badly about yourself when you recognised that you had done something that merited criticism?

[*Having discovered that the issue is self-criticism when he receives criticism from someone else that he agrees with, I then ask for a time when he did not criticise himself under such circumstances.*]

Client: Yes, I remember a few months ago, I did something that I thought would be criticised by my boss and I thought, 'You know what, yes, I could have done better but I'm not a robot, I am going to cut myself some slack.'

Windy: And what was the result of you thinking that?

Client: Yeah, I felt much better.

Windy: If every time you were criticised by someone and you thought that the criticism had some merit, you stood back, acknowledged that you could have done better, but reminded yourself that you weren't a robot and that you were going to cut yourself some slack, what would the consequence of doing that be for you?

[*Note that I am using the client's words in outlining the solution that they had already used. It is important that you don't change your client's language here.*]

Client: Then I would handle criticism much better.

Windy: From my perspective, the interesting thing is that you had already solved your problem but hadn't realised it. What's your learning from this?

Client: What I need to do is to remember that I already have a solution to my problem and that I need to use.

Windy: Shall we discuss an action plan to help you do that?

Client: Great idea.

See another example in the section below entitled, 'Helping the Client to Develop Confidence by Doing Things Unconfidently'.

7. Helping the Client to Understand the Problem before Suggesting 'Tips and Techniques'

As I explained in Chapter 7, it is my practice in ONEplus therapy to send the client a pre-session questionnaire to complete, designed to help them prepare for the session to get the most from it. Once they have completed it, I invite them to return the questionnaire to me so that I can also prepare myself for the session. Most people (but not all) who access ONEplus therapy seek help for an emotional or behavioural problem with which they feel stuck and state that they want to learn some 'tips and techniques' to help them deal with their problem. When this happens, I ask them whether it would be better for them to learn such 'tips and techniques' based on a complete understanding of their problem or without such understanding. They invariably reply that the former would be much better.

As a result, what we do is understand the factors that account for the client's problem, the factors that explain why the client is maintaining the problem, albeit unwittingly and other relevant contextual factors. From such an understanding, a possible solution to the client's problem will be more readily discerned, and this can be put within the frame of a 'tip' or 'technique' if the client resonates with such terms.

8. Helping the Client to Develop Confidence by Doing Things Unconfidently

It happens quite frequently that the client's nominated problem is linked to their lack of confidence in doing something. Consequently, they decide not to do it. I have found it useful to ask them about their previous experience of dealing with not being confident as a way of helping them to see the lack of confidence in a new light. Here is a typical exchange.

Windy: So, you are saying that because you lack confidence, you don't do presentations to your team, but as a result, you may be harming your promotion prospects. Is that right?

Client: Yes.

Windy: Have you ever had the experience of not being confident about doing something, doing it and then ending up being confident at it?

Client: Yes … about driving.

Windy: Please tell me about it.

Client: Well, before I started to drive, I wasn't very confident, but then after some lessons and practice, I developed confidence, and now I would say I am a confident driver.

Windy: What relevance does that process have for you in developing confidence about giving presentations to your team?

Client: I can't expect to be confident at the beginning. But if I do some presentations to my team, even though I am not confident and I get some feedback, I can become confident the more presentations I give.

Windy: Are you prepared to do that?

Client: It's worth a try.

9. Helping the Client to View Discomfort as a Friend and Not as an Enemy

We live in an age where we are encouraged to be comfortable. When someone says that they are not uncomfortable with something that another person has done, they often mean that they want the other person to stop whatever it is they have been doing that has made the first person feel uncomfortable.

However, change frequently involves your client feeling discomfort partly because they are beginning to do something they are not used to. We often refer to this as coming out of one's comfort zone. I had wanted to do a bungee jump for a long time, and finally, the opportunity came when I was in New Zealand in 2019. So, I decided to take advantage of this opportunity. Was I uncomfortable? Definitely. But I did not let the discomfort that I felt stop me from doing something that it was important for me to do.

This is the important point. Discomfort is not universally good or universally bad, so I have found it valuable in ONEplus therapy to help clients distinguish between discomfort they need to experience because it helps them achieve their problem-related goals and discomfort that is not relevant to reaching their goals. In the first case, I help clients see that such discomfort is their friend, not their enemy.

10. Helping the Client Distinguish Between Enthusiasm-Based Motivation, Fear-based Motivation and Reason-Based Motivation

Sometimes a client may say that they lack the motivation to do something. In my experience, it is important to understand what they mean by this statement. First, it may be an indication that the client is depressed. If this is the case, then you need to help the client to understand that they are depressed and enquire what they are depressed about (see the section below entitled 'Helping the Client to Understand and Deal with Depression'). However, taking 'lack of motivation' at face value, it is important to determine what kind of motivation they lack.

A client means 'enthusiasm-based motivation' when they say such things as 'I didn't feel like doing it' or 'I didn't do it because I lacked motivation'. So, 'enthusiasm-based motivation' is the 'in the moment' enthusiasm or drive to do a task. It is a proximal factor, meaning something that is close or near. In the above examples, the person believes that if they lack the drive or enthusiasm in the moment to do something, then this explains why they did not do it. They will wait to experience 'enthusiasm-based motivation' and then do the task. However, because they continue to lack 'enthusiasm-based motivation', they postpone the task until there is a real risk of suffering negative consequences if they continue to delay. What the person then does is to do the task because they experience 'fear-based motivation' – they are fearful of experiencing the negative consequences of failing to do the task. In such circumstances, the person is still motivated by a proximal factor, but it is fear rather than the absence of enthusiasm. Here, the person comes to believe they need the fear to do the task (see also the section below on 'Helping the Client to Understand and Deal with Procrastination').

By contrast, 'reason-based motivation' refers to the client having a good reason or set of good reasons to do the task. These reasons are a distal factor, meaning something that is further away in space or time. To assess reason-based motivation, you can ask such questions as:

- 'Why is it important to you to do the task?'
- 'What reasons do you have for doing the task?'

The client's responses will tell you if the stated reasons are good enough, from their perspective, to do the task.

The more the reasons are important to the person and the more closely they align with their client's values, the more motivating they will be from a reason-based perspective. In this case, I would refer to such 'reason-based motivation' as 'inner-directed and value-founded'. This type of 'reason-based motivation' is strong and usually motivating when considered.

When in answer to the above questions, the person responds that they would be doing the task for others and not for themself or that the reasons they give are not aligned with their values, then I refer to such 'reason-based motivation' as 'outer-directed and not founded on values'. This latter type of 'reason-based motivation' is weak and usually not motivating when considered.

Having outlined the three types of motivation (including the two sub-types of 'reason-based motivation'), I discuss with the client which type of motivation explains their problem and which one would provide a solution to their problem. This often results in the person coming to see that if they want to do the task at hand, they need to:

- Remind themself that while it would be nice to have 'enthusiasm-based' motivation before they did the task, it is not necessary for them to experience it and that they can start the task without it.

- Understand that once they begin the task without enthusiasm, they will often experience such enthusiasm once they have become involved in doing the task.

- Review the inner-directed, value-founded reasons for doing the task and keep these reasons to the forefront of their mind.

- Realise that it will be strange and uncomfortable for them to take action without 'enthusiasm-based motivation' and 'fear-based motivation', but the more they do so, the more familiar and comfortable they will feel acting on inner-directed, value-founded ('reason-based') motivation.

11. Helping the Client to Distinguish Between Unhealthy and Healthy Negative Emotions

One of the most useful concepts I use in ONEplus therapy is the distinction between unhealthy negative emotions (UNEs) and healthy negative emotions (HNEs). When a client nominates a problem to discuss in ONEplus therapy, there is usually an adversity at the heart of the problem. Examples of such adversities are rejection, criticism, failure and threat. Since an adversity is negative, then even if the person is dealing constructively with the adversity, they will feel negatively about it, but this negative emotion, although negative in feeling tone, will be healthy in effect. Thus, a healthy negative emotion will be associated with constructive behaviour and thinking that will be realistic, balanced and non-ruminative in nature.

By contrast, when the person is dealing unconstructively with the same adversity, they will also feel negatively, but this negative emotion, although again in feeling tone will be unhealthy in effect. Thus, an unhealthy negative emotion will be associated with unconstructive behaviour and thinking that will be highly negatively distorted and ruminative in nature.

Thus, when a person wants to feel neutral or OK about an adversity, I explain why this is unrealistic. I then help them see that when they face the adversity that features in their nominated problem, they choose between experiencing a healthy negative emotion or an unhealthy negative emotion about the adversity. Table 2 lists common adversities and the unhealthy and healthy negative emotions that are associated with these adversities.

12. Getting to the Heart of the Matter

In my experience of practising ONEplus therapy, it is worth spending time with the client to discover what is the heart of their problem. In supervising people learning to become ONEplus therapists, this is something that they struggle with. They think they should get to the point very quickly because they may have only one session with the client. As a result, they do not get as much personalised information about the client's nominated problem as is needed. As a result, the person gets some help from the session but not as much help as they could have gotten if the therapist had spent more time assessing the problem more carefully.

Table 2 Adversities with associated unhealthy and healthy

Adversity	Negative Emotion	
	Unhealthy	Healthy
• Threat	Anxiety	Concern
• Loss • Failure • Undeserved plight (experienced by self or others)	Depression	Sadness
• Breaking your moral code • Failing to abide by your moral code • Hurting someone	Guilt	Remorse
• Doing something you wished you had not done • Not doing something you wished you had done	Unhealthy Regret	Healthy Regret
• Falling very short of your ideal in a social context • Others judging you negatively	Shame	Disappointment
• The other is less invested in your relationship than you • Someone betrays you or lets you down and you think you do not deserve such treatment	Hurt	Sorrow
• You or another transgresses a personal rule • Another disrespects you • Frustration	Unhealthy Anger	Healthy Anger
• Someone poses a threat to a valued relationship • You experience uncertainty related to this threat	Unhealthy Jealousy	Healthy Jealousy
• Others have what you value and lack	Unhealthy Envy	Healthy Envy

Getting to the heart of the matter involves you, the therapist, helping the client to be clear about their most prominent disturbed emotion and what they were most disturbed about. I refer you to Table 2 (see above) for the framework that I hold in mind when striving to get to the heart of the matter of the client's problem. If I am having difficulty helping my client and me to find out what they were most disturbed about, I use a method which I call 'Windy's Magic Question'.

Using Windy's Magic Question

When you use the 'magic question' technique to identify what your client finds most problematic, I suggest that you take the following steps:

Step 1. Ask your client to select a specific example of their problem and succinctly describe the situation.

Step 2. Focus on the situation in which your client disturbed themself (i.e. where they experienced their predominant unhealthy negative emotion).

Peter focused on the following situation in which he felt ashamed: 'I lost my temper with my cousin.'

Step 3. Ask your client first to imagine that the situation cannot be changed. Then, ask them to identify the one factor that would get rid of or significantly reduce their unhealthy negative emotion in the situation.

Peter identified the following factor which would have reduced his feelings of shame: Having a good reason for losing my temper with my cousin.

Step 4. The opposite is probably what the client was most disturbed about.

What Peter was most disturbed about: Losing my temper with my cousin for no good reason.

When using the magic question technique do not allow your client to change the actual situation at step 1. Doing so will not help you and your client to identify the adversity at the heart of their problem.

13. Encouraging the Client to Develop a Flexible Attitude

One of the significant ideas that inform my practice in therapy in general and ONEplus therapy, in particular, stems from the work of Albert Ellis. as detailed in Rational Emotive Behaviour Therapy, a therapeutic approach that he originally developed in the late 1950s (see Ellis, 1994). When using some of Ellis's ideas in ONEplus therapy, I have found it useful to change the language to make them more accessible to clients. One such concept is that of 'attitude' which I use instead of belief. An attitude is 'an enduring pattern of evaluative responses towards a person, object, or issue' (Colman, 2015). Rather than use Ellis's terminology, where he distinguishes between irrational and rational beliefs, I use the more understandable and contemporary distinction between a rigid and flexible attitude (Dryden, 2016).

By a rigid attitude, I refer to a situation where a person holds an attitude that they must get what they want or that they must not get what they don't want in some vital sphere of their life. By a flexible attitude, I refer to a situation where a person holds an attitude that they don't have to get what they want or don't have to be spared from getting what they don't want in the same vital sphere of their life.

Let me give an example of the distinction between a rigid and flexible attitude in a common problem for which a client seeks ONEplus therapy – dealing with criticism. When the person has difficulties in dealing with criticism, it is clear that it is important to them that they are not criticised. This desire is common to both rigid and flexible attitudes. Where they differ is that when the person holds a rigid attitude towards criticism, they take their desire and make it rigid, whereas when they hold a flexible attitude, they keep their desire flexible. This is shown in Figure 2.

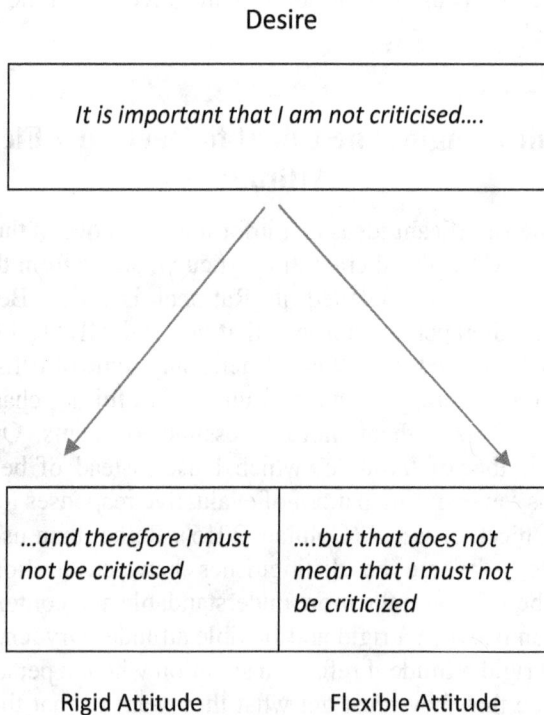

Desire

It is important that I am not criticised....

...and therefore I must not be criticised

....but that does not mean that I must not be criticized

Rigid Attitude   Flexible Attitude

Figure 2 Difference between a rigid and flexible attitude

Once the client can see the distinction between these attitudes, I ask them which one they want to take forward. They invariably select the flexible attitude, so we discuss how the person can do this.

14. Helping the Client to Develop an Attitude of Bearability

Sometimes at the heart of a client's nominated problem lies an attitude of unbearability.   The healthy alternative to this attitude is what I term an attitude of bearability. In Table 3, I outline the components of each attitude.

Table 3 Difference between attitudes of unbearability and bearability

Struggle Component

It is a struggle for me to bear being criticised ….	
Attitude of Unbearability	Attitude of Bearability
…and I can't bear it	… but I can bear it It is worth bearing I am worth bearing it for I am willing to bear it I am going to bear it Taking action in ways that are consistent with the attitude of bearability

Once the client sees the relevance of developing an attitude of bearability, I help them to put this into their own words so that it forms the basis of the solution to their nominated problem.

15. Helping the Client to Take the Horror Out of Badness

Clients may mention that they 'catastrophise' their experience, which they think is a core component of their nominated problem. If so, my strategy is to help them take the horror out of badness, not the badness out of badness. The latter is known as a non-awfulising attitude and is the healthy alternative to an awfulising attitude. In Table 4, I outline the components of each attitude.

Table 4 Difference between attitudes of awfulising and non-awfulising

Evaluation of Badness Component

It is bad if I am criticised ….	
Awfulizing Attitude	Non-Awfulising Attitude
…and therefore, it is the end of the world	…. but it is not the end of the world

Again, once the client sees the relevance of developing a non-awfulising attitude, I help them to put this into their own words so that it forms the basis of the solution to their nominated problem.

16. Helping the Client to Develop an Attitude of Unconditional Self-Acceptance

A number of clients present with problems of low self-esteem. Obviously, you cannot help them solve such problems in one session, but what you can do as a ONEplus therapist is offer your client a framework to deal with their self-esteem issue going forward. In this respect, I suggest that the client consider using the following framework to develop an attitude of unconditional self-acceptance instead of a self-devaluation attitude (see Table 5).

Table 5 Difference between attitudes of self-devaluation and unconditional self-acceptance

Negative Evaluation of a Part of Self

It is bad that I performed poorly, for which I have been criticised ….	
Self-Devaluation Attitude	Attitude of Unconditional Self-Acceptance
…and this proves that I am worthless	…. but this does not prove that I am worthless. It proves that I am a unique, complex unrateable, fallible human being capable of acting well, poorly and neutrally

As before, once the client sees the relevance of developing an attitude of unconditional self-acceptance, I help them to put this into their own words so that it forms the basis of the solution to their nominated problem. I also use Figure 1 (see the section above entitled 'Utilise the visual medium as well as the verbal medium') to demonstrate the same point but visually. This figure shows the 'Big I – little I' technique, which demonstrates that our 'self' (or 'Big I') comprises many different aspects or 'little i's' and that any of its aspects cannot define the self.

17. Helping the Client to Develop an Attitude of Unconditional Other-Acceptance

If a client has an anger problem towards another person or group of people then it is likely that a rigid attitude and an attitude of other-devaluation underpin such anger. In my view, helping them to address their anger problem involves them developing a flexible attitude towards the other's behaviour (see the section on 'Encouraging the Client to Develop a Flexible Attitude' above) and an attitude of unconditional other-acceptance (see Table 6, next page).

18. Helping the Client to Accept Reality

I had written 16,000 words of this book and was feeling good because I was enjoying writing it and was ahead of schedule. Then, when I came to work on the draft, I found that the Word file was corrupted, and I could not find a way of opening it. I purchased an online tool that claimed would help me recover what I wrote. However, all it did was wipe the USB drive clean, and I lost the file altogether. And … I had forgotten to back up my work! How did I respond? I accepted reality. This meant the following:

Table 6 Difference between attitudes of other-devaluation and unconditional other-acceptance

Negative Evaluation of a Part of Self

It is bad that the person acted poorly ….	
Other-Devaluation Attitude	Attitude of Unconditional Other-Acceptance
… and this proves that they are worthless	…. but this does not prove that they are worthless. It proves that they are a unique, complex unrateable, fallible human being capable of acting well, poorly and neutrally

- I acknowledged that I had lost my file and had not backed up my work.
- I really did not like that this happened.
- I recognised that, unfortunately, all the conditions were in place for this to occur and that things did not have to be different. Indeed, they had to be the way they were. Why? Because they were. Reality has to be reality!
- I decided to email myself the work from now on, and I would back up my work to two different files. This worked in that my file did not get corrupted again and if it had been, I had copies of the work to hand.

When appropriate, I use the above schema with clients if they are interested in hearing what I have to say about accepting reality.

19. Using Windy's Review Assessment Procedure (WRAP)

When I have asked my client if they are interested on my 'take' on their problem and they reply in the affirmative, I offer them an attitude-based perspective informed by Rational Emotive Behaviour Therapy (REBT). I use what I call Windy's Review Assessment Procedure (WRAP) to assess the attitude that underpins the client's nominated problem. I will use the example of Peter to show you how to use this method of assessing attitudes. As such, I will talk to Peter directly.

1. At this point, we know that your emotion is shame and that your adversity is 'I lost my temper with my cousin for no good reason.'

    We also know your preference, which is, 'I would have preferred it if I hadn't lost my temper with my cousin for no good reason.'

    [I know this because I use REBT theory to guide my work (Dryden, 2022c). This states that whenever a client has an emotional problem, this is based on a preference that they have either for something to happen or for something not to happen (as in Peter's case).]

2. What we don't know yet is which of two attitudes your feelings of shame are based on – a rigid or flexible attitude[37]. So are your feelings of shame based on Attitude #1, 'I would have preferred it if I hadn't lost my temper with my cousin for no good reason and therefore I

---

[37] The WRAP technique can also be used to identify extreme attitudes and their non-extreme attitude alternatives (see Dryden, 2022c).

absolutely should not have done so' or Attitude #2: 'I would have preferred it if I hadn't lost my temper with my cousin for no good reason, but I don't have to behave in the way I would have preferred.'

[*If Peter does not see that his feelings of shame are based on Attitude #1, I would discuss this with him until he understands this 'rigid attitude – unhealthy negative emotion' connection.*]

3. Now answer the following question: 'If you had a strong conviction in Attitude #2, how would you feel about losing your temper with your cousin for no good reason'?

    [*If Peter does not say 'disappointed' or some suitable synonym, I would discuss this with him until he understands this 'flexible attitude – healthy negative emotion' connection.*]

4. You now see clearly that your feelings of shame are based on your rigid attitude ("I would have preferred it if I hadn't lost my temper with my cousin for no good reason and therefore I absolutely should not have done so') and that your healthy feelings of disappointment are based on your flexible attitude ('I would have preferred it if I hadn't lost my temper with my cousin for no good reason, but I don't have to behave in the way I would have preferred').

5. Does it make sense for you to set disappointment as your emotional goal in this situation and see that developing conviction in your flexible attitude ('I would have preferred it if I hadn't lost my temper with my cousin for no good reason, but I don't have to behave in the way I would have preferred') is the best way of achieving this goal?

    [*If Peter has any doubts, reservations or objections todoing so, I would discuss them with him.*]

20. Helping Clients to Examine Their Attitudes

In ONEplus therapy where time is at a premium, I am looking for an efficient way of helping my client to stand back and examine the two sets of attitudes that underpin their disturbed responses to the adversity featured in their problem (rigid/extreme attitudes[38]) and their healthy responses to the same adversity (flexible/non-extreme attitudes[39]). In this section, I will discuss two ways of doing this: a) using the choice-based examination method and b) using persuasive arguments.

The Choice-Based Examination Method

You can employ the choice-based method with your client's rigid attitude and the flexible alternative to attitude and/or the most relevant extreme attitude and the non-extreme alternative to this attitude. While using it, you ask your client to focus on both attitudes and choose which is true and which is false, which is logical and which is illogical and which is healthy and which is unhealthy, and to give reasons for their choice.

Using the choice-based examination method with rigid and flexible attitudes

When using this method with my client's rigid and flexible attitudes, I encourage them to focus on both attitudes and ask them the following questions.

- Which of these two attitudes is true or consistent with reality and which is false or inconsistent with reality and why?

---

[38] These extreme attitudes are: attitudes of unbearability, awfulising attitudes and devaluation attitudes (see Tables 3–6).
[39] These extreme attitudes are: attitudes of bearability, non-awfulising attitudes and unconditional acceptance attitudes (see Tables 3–6).

- Which of these two attitudes is logical or sensible and which is illogical or nonsensical and why?
- Which of these two attitudes is largely helpful to you and which is largely unhelpful to you and why?
- Which of these attitudes do you want to choose to develop going forward and why?

Using Persuasive Arguments

In my opinion, the 'Choice-Based Examination Method' is the most structured way of helping clients to examine both their rigid and flexible attitudes and their extreme and non-extreme attitudes at the same time, However, it is also important that you help your client to develop their own ways of examining these attitudes focusing on using arguments that are persuasive to them. Here are a few examples of implementing this more creative approach to examining attitudes.

Teach your children

Here you take an attitude pair (e.g. a rigid attitude and flexible attitude) and you ask your client to decide which of the attitudes they would like to teach a child or a group of children for whom they have responsibility and/or about whom they care. In teaching the child(ren), please be sure to ask your client to explain the reasons for their choice in terms that the child(ren) can understand.

Which attitude would you like to have been taught?

Take the attitude and ask your client which of these two attitudes they would have liked to have been taught growing up and why. Also, ask them to make clear why they would not have liked to have been taught the other attitude.

Use diagrams

Some clients are more receptive to points being made visually rather than verbally. If so, draw a diagram that would help your client to accept the flexible/non-extreme attitude rather than the rigid/extreme or attitude. An example of this is shown in Figure 1[40] which shows the 'Big I – little i' technique. As described before, this technique shows that the 'self' (or 'Big I') comprises many different aspects or 'little i's'. It also illustrates that the self cannot be defined by its aspects.

21. Helping the Client to Understand and Deal with Anxiety

In this and the following sections of this chapter, I will discuss what I have to offer clients seeking help with specific emotional problems and procrastination. Again, you need to note that I will only offer a client my perspective when they are clearly struggling to understand or deal with their nominated emotional problem. So, as mentioned before, when this happens, I will ask my client if they are interested in my take on their nominated emotional problem and how they can deal with. If they are interested, I will share it. If they are not, I won't.

Of all the emotional problems that people seek help for from ONEplus therapy, anxiety is probably the most frequent. It strikes me that many clients know very little about anxiety that will help them deal with their anxiety problems. So here are some ideas that I have found useful to introduce into my conversation with clients that can help them understand and deal with this common emotional problem.

---

[40] See the section in this chapter entitled, 'Utilise the visual medium as well as the verbal medium'.

- Anxiety[41] has two major components. First, it is based on a set of rigid and extreme attitudes that the person holds towards something that they deem to be threatening. Second, it is based on the person's appraisal that they won't be able to deal with the threat. It follows that you may need to help them with the first, second or both components.

- The healthy alternative to anxiety is non-anxious concern. It is not the absence of anxiety or a less intense form of anxiety. Non-anxious concern also has two major components. First, it is based on a set of flexible/non-extreme attitudes that the person holds towards the same threat as in anxiety. Second, it is based on the person's appraisal that they will be able to deal with the threat.

- Quite often, people make themselves disturbed about their anxiety (e.g., ashamed, depressed, guilty etc.)[42] If this is the case with your client, you need to decide whether to focus on their original anxiety or their meta-emotional disturbance. You may or may not have time to address both in the first (and perhaps only) session of ONEplus therapy. When helping your client to deal with their disturbed feelings about anxiety, you can help them in three ways. Help them understand that (i) the feeling of anxiety is painful but usually not dangerous; (ii) they can bear feeling anxious even though they think that they cannot bear it, and iii) anxiety is a sign that they are a fallible human being who is holding a rigid and extreme attitude towards threat. It is not evidence that they are a weak person.

- Attempts to eliminate anxiety only serve to maintain or increase it. Realistic, mindful acceptance of anxiety is the

---

[41] In this section, I will be discussing anxiety, which is psychological in nature. Sometimes, anxiety is related more to medical issues.

[42] When a person disturbs themself about their original disturbance, this is known as meta-emotional disturbance.

healthy alternative to elimination. This involves your client acknowledging that they feel anxiety and that it is unpleasant. They then decide to let the anxious feelings remain so that they can deal with them effectively.

- Anxiety thrives on your client's attempts to avoid and withdraw from threat. Instead, they need to face the threat and deal with it effectively.

- Anxiety loves closets. Thus, your client needs to come out of their closet and, as above, face and deal with the threat.

Helping the Client to Deal Healthily with the Issue of Loss of Control

One of the most common threats people experience when anxious is loss of control. I have found it useful to help clients who experience such anxiety to consider the following:

- It is important that you are clear about what you are in control of (largely yourself) and what you are not in control of (largely others and events involving others).

- If you hold a rigid and extreme attitude towards loss of self-control this will lead you to think that you will lose complete control of yourself if you begin to lose such control.

- If you hold a flexible and non-extreme attitude towards loss of self-control this will lead you to focus on how to respond when you begin to lose such control. You will tend not to think you will lose complete control of yourself.

Helping the Client to Deal Healthily with Uncertainty

Another common threat that people experience when they are anxious is uncertainty. I have found it useful to help clients who experience such anxiety to consider the following:

- Uncertainty in the face of threat does not on its own lead to anxiety.

- If you hold a rigid and extreme attitude towards such uncertainty this will lead to anxiety. This attitude will lead you to think that if you do not know you are safe, then you are in danger.

- If you hold a flexible and non-extreme attitude towards such uncertainty this will lead to non-anxious concern. This attitude will lead you to think that you are probably safe even if you do not know for certain that you are.

- Thus, it is quite probable that you are safe even when you are facing uncertainty. Uncertainty is not a sign of danger. It is a sign that you are in a state of not knowing. This may be an unpleasant state, but that is all that it is.

- Only seek reassurance if you are able to be reassured in the longer term (i.e. you are re-assurable). Continually seeking reassurance when you are not re-assurable, will maintain your anxiety problem.

22. Helping the Client to Understand and Deal with Depression

After anxiety, depression is the next most common emotional problem that people seek help for from ONEplus therapy.[43] Again, many clients know very little about depression that will help them deal with their problems of depression and low mood.

---

[43] In this section, I will discuss what might be called non-clinical depression. This is depression that will respond to psychological intervention.

So here are some ideas that I have found useful to introduce into my conversation with clients that can help them understand and deal with depression.

- When people are non-clinically depressed, they tend to be depressed about a loss, a failure or an undeserved plight experienced by self or others.

- Such depression is based on a set of rigid and extreme attitudes that the person holds towards loss/ failure/undeserved plight.

- The healthy alternative to depression is non-depressed sadness. This is based on a set of flexible and non-extreme attitudes that the person holds towards loss/failure/undeserved plight.

- Another way of looking at depression is to see that this emotion may be sociotropic or autonomous (Beck, Epstein & Harrison, 1983). When it is sociotopic in nature, the person is heavily invested in relationships and holds a set of rigid and extreme attitudes towards loss, failure or undeserved plight with respect to these relationships. When it is autonomous in nature, the person is heavily invested in autonomy, personal achievement and control and holds a set of rigid and extreme attitudes towards loss, failure or undeserved plight with respect to these conditions.

- The healthy alternative to sociotropic and autonomous depression is sociotropic and autonomous non-depressed sadness. In both, the person holds a set of flexible and non-extreme attitudes towards loss/failure/undeserved plight.

- When a person is depressed, this affects their behaviour. They tend to withdraw into themself, become inactive and refrain from engaging in activities that they previously found pleasurable and which gave them a sense of mastery. Part of helping clients with depression is to encourage them to help them become more active and re-engage with these mastery and pleasure activities. This may be best done before helping them with attitude change or afterwards. People who are sad, but not depressed tend to stay active.

- When a person is depressed, this affects their subsequent thinking. They tend to think that things are hopeless, and that they are helpless to deal with life. They also tend to engage in depressive rumination. Helping people deal with the depressed thinking accompanying their depressed behaviour involves first encouraging them to trace such thinking back to the rigid and extreme attitudes that are the toot of their depressed feelings and then to examine them and help them change these attitudes to their flexible and non-extreme attitudinal counterparts. After you have done this, you are in a better position to help them stand back, deal with their hopeless and helpless thinking and help them to disengage from depressive rumination. This is where mindfulness can be particularly helpful.

It is important to bear in mind that a person must be reasonably active to engage in such cognitive techniques. If they are not, you first need to help them to become more behaviourally active.

23. Helping the Client to Understand and Deal with Guilt

Here are some ideas that I have found useful to introduce into my conversation with clients that can help them understand and deal with guilt.

- When a person experiences guilt, they hold a rigid and self-devaluation attitude towards one or more of the following adversities: (i) I have broken my moral code (a sin of commission); (ii) I have failed to live up to my moral code (a sin of omission); (iii) hurting others (e.g., 'I absolutely should not have hurt my parents' feelings, and I am a bad person for doing so'). When the person feels guilt, behaviourally, they will punish themself and beg for rather than ask for forgiveness. Guilt will also inhibit assertive behaviour. Cognitively, the person will engage in guilt-related rumination and take too much responsibility than is warranted for their behaviour and assign others who were involved too little responsibility than is warranted.

- The healthy alternative to guilt is guilt-free remorse.[44]

- When the person experiences guilt-free remorse about the same adversities, then they hold a flexible attitude and an attitude of unconditional self-acceptance towards these adversities (e.g., 'I really wish I had not hurt my parents' feelings, but sadly I am not immune from doing so and neither do I have to have such immunity. I am not bad for doing so; rather, I am a complex, unique and fallible human being who acted badly on this occasion, but capable of acting well'). When the person feels guilt-free remorse, behaviourally, they might take a penalty for their behaviour, but will not punish themself. They will ask for but will not beg for forgiveness. They will be able to assert themself. Cognitively, the person will take the appropriate amount of responsibility for their behaviour and assign the appropriate amount of responsibility to others who were involved. They will not engage in guilt-based rumination.

---

[44] We lack universally accepted terms to describe healthy negative emotions (HNEs). Thus, what I will do in this book is refer to the terms that I typically use. However, in ONEplus therapy, using terms that make more sense to clients is vital, and if a client does not resonate with a particular HNE term, I suggest that you employ the term that does resonate with them.

- If the person is interested, I will help them change their rigid/extreme attitudes to their flexible/non-extreme counterparts and help them think and act in ways that will support the development of these attitudes.

24. Helping the Client to Understand and Deal with Unhealthy Regret

Here are some ideas that I have found useful to introduce into my conversation with clients that can help them deal with unhealthy regret (Dryden, 2023).

- When a person experiences unhealthy regret, they hold a rigid and extreme attitude towards one of the following two adversities: (i) I acted in a way that I wish I hadn't and (ii) I failed to act in a way that I wish I had (e.g., 'I did not take that job when it was offered to me years ago and I absolutely should have done so. It's terrible that I turned that job down').

- When a person holds such a rigid and extreme attitude, they think their life would have been much better if they had chosen differently. They also engage in what I call unhealthy regret-related rumination. In their mind, they try to undo what they did or what they did not do but fail. However, such failure leads to more rumination. They also keep searching in their mind for a good enough reason to explain their past decision but fail to find it. Rather than give up these pursuits, they keep trying to find answers that will satisfy them through such rumination. Both of these ruminative strategies are doomed to fail because rigid and extreme attitudes underpin such thinking.

- The healthy alternative to unhealthy regret is healthy regret.

- When a person experiences healthy regret, they hold a flexible and non-extreme attitude towards the same two adversities: (i) I acted in a way that I wish I hadn't and (ii) I failed to act in a way that I wish I had (e.g., 'I did not take that job when it was offered to me years ago. I wish I had done so, but that does not mean that I absolutely should have done so. It's unfortunate that I turned that job down, but not terrible').

- When a person holds this flexible and non-extreme attitude, they think their life may have been much better if they had chosen differently, but they also recognise that it could have been worse, or it may have made no difference. They tend not to engage in rumination. They recognise that their past action (or inaction) was due to how they thought then and that there is no way to undo that now. All they can do now is learn from that experience and use that learning to guide their future decisions.

- If the person is interested, I will help them change their rigid/extreme attitudes to their flexible/non-extreme counterparts and help them think and act in ways that will support the development of these attitudes.

25. Helping the Client to Understand and Deal with Shame

Here are some ideas that I have found useful to introduce into my conversation with clients that can help them deal with shame.

- When a person experiences shame, they hold a rigid and self-devaluation attitude towards one or more of the following adversities: (i) I have fallen very short of my ideal, usually in a social context and (ii) others have judged me negatively when I have fallen short of my ideal (e.g., 'I said something silly in a work presentation which I absolutely should not have done. There is something wrong with me.'). Behaviourally, when the person experiences shame, they will tend to hide away from others and avoid situations where they may experience this emotion. Cognitively, the person will tend to overestimate the amount and extent of the negative evaluation they will get from others and will engage in shame-based rumination.

- The healthy alternative to shame is shame-free disappointment.

- When the person experiences shame-free disappointment about the same adversities, then they hold a flexible attitude and an attitude of unconditional self-acceptance towards these adversities (e.g., 'I really wish I had not said something silly in a work presentation, but that does not mean that I absolutely should not have done so. There may have been something wrong with what I said, but there is nothing wrong with me. I am a fallible human capable of acting in many ways'). Behaviourally, when the person experiences shame-free disappointment, they will face others rather than hide away from them. Cognitively, the person will make realistic inferences about the amount and extent of negative evaluations they will get from others, but will not engage in shame-based rumination.

- Again, if the person is interested, I will help them change their rigid/extreme attitudes to their flexible/non-extreme counterparts and help them think and act in ways that will support the development of these attitudes.

26. Helping the Client to Understand and Deal with Unhealthy Anger

Here are some ideas that I have found useful to introduce into my conversation with clients that can help them understand and deal with unhealthy anger.

- When a person experiences unhealthy anger, they hold a rigid and extreme attitude towards one or more of the following adversities: (i) Another person (or you, yourself) has transgressed an important personal rule; (ii) Another person has disrespected you and (iii) You have been frustrated in your pursuit towards (e.g., 'You put me down in public which you absolutely should not have done. You are bad for doing so'). When you experience unhealthy anger, you feel like attacking the object of your anger and engage in revenge-based rumination.

- The healthy alternative to unhealthy anger is healthy anger.

- When the person experiences healthy anger about the same adversities, then they hold a flexible attitude and a non-extreme attitude towards these adversities (e.g., 'I really wish you had not put me down in public, but this does not mean that you absolutely should not have done so. What you did was bad, but you are not a bad person. You are a fallible human being who did the wrong thing'). When you experience healthy anger, you want to assert yourself with the other rather than attack them and you don't engage in revenge-based rumination.

- Again, if the person is interested, I will help them change their rigid/extreme attitudes to their flexible/non-extreme counterparts and help them think and act in ways that will support the development of these attitudes.

27. Helping the Client to Understand and Deal with Hurt

Here are some ideas that I have found useful to introduce into my conversation with clients that can help them understand and deal with hurt.

- When a person experiences hurt, they hold a rigid and extreme attitude towards one of the following adversities: (i) Another person whom you value is less invested in your relationship with them than you are; (ii) Another person whom you value has let you down or betrayed you, and you think that you are undeserving of such treatment (e.g., 'My best friend doesn't care about me as much as I care about her because she went out with another friend and did not invite me. She must care about me as much as I care about her, and it is terrible that she doesn't'). When you experience hurt. You tend to sulk and engage in hurt-based rumination.

- The healthy alternative to hurt is hurt-free sorrow.

- When the person experiences hurt-free sorrow about the same adversities, they hold a flexible and non-extreme attitude towards these adversities (e.g., 'I really wish my best friend cares about me as much as I care about her, but sadly she does not have to do so. It is bad that she doesn't but not terrible. When you experience hurt-free sorrow, you want to discuss how you feel with the other rather than sulk and you don't engage in hurt-based rumination.

- Once again, if the person is interested, I will help them change their rigid/extreme attitudes to their flexible/non-extreme counterparts and help them think and act in ways that will support the development of these attitudes.

28. Helping the Client to Understand and Deal with Unhealthy Jealousy

Here are some ideas that I have found useful to introduce into my conversation with clients that can help them understand and deal with unhealthy jealousy.

- When a person experiences unhealthy jealousy, they hold a rigid and extreme attitude towards one or both of the following adversities: (i) They think that another person poses a risk to a valued relationship and (ii) they experience uncertainty related to the first threat (e.g., 'I want to know that my partner is not interested in any of the men she works with and therefore I have to know this. I can't bear not knowing'). When a person experiences unhealthy jealousy, they tend to take action to prevent what they fear and think that if they don't, then what they fear will happen, and also that uncertainty means that something bad is going on.

- The healthy alternative to unhealthy jealousy is healthy jealousy (sometimes called relationship concern).

- When the person experiences healthy jealousy (or relationship concern) about the same adversities, they hold a flexible and non-extreme attitude towards these adversities (e.g., 'I want to know that my partner is not interested in any of the men she works with, but I don't have to know this. It's a struggle not knowing, but I can bear it and it's worth bearing'). When a person experiences healthy jealousy, they don't take action to prevent what they are concerned about and they think that probably nothing bad will happen if they don't. They also think that uncertainty does not mean that something bad is going on. In this and other matters they decide to go along with probability.

- When a self-devaluation attitude is a prominent feature of unhealthy jealousy, I discuss the importance of developing an attitude of unconditional self-acceptance as a solution.

- Yet again, if the person is interested, I will help them change their rigid/extreme attitudes to their flexible/non-extreme counterparts and help them think and act in ways that will support the development of these attitudes.

29. Helping the Client to Understand and Deal with Unhealthy Envy

Here are some ideas that I have found useful to introduce into my conversation with clients that can help them understand and deal with unhealthy envy.

- When a person experiences unhealthy envy, they hold a rigid and extreme attitude towards another person having something or somebody in their life that the person prizes but lacks (e.g., 'My friend has just got a new job, and I wish I had what she has and therefore I must have what she has, and I can't bear the resulting deprivation'). When a person experiences unhealthy envy, behaviourally they take desperate steps to get what they don't have and may try to spoil in action and/or in words what the other person has and enjoys or they may devalue the other person to others. Their unhealthy envy-influenced thinking is ruminative in nature and is focused on how to get what the other person has or on how to spoil things for the other person.

- The healthy alternative to unhealthy envy is healthy envy.

- When the person experiences healthy envy about the same adversity, they hold a flexible and non-extreme attitude towards this adversity (e.g., 'My friend has just got a new job, and I wish I had what she has, but I don't have to have it. I don't like the resulting deprivation, but I can bear it and it is worth bearing'). When a person experiences healthy envy, they still might strive to get what the other person has, but only if they truly want it and not because the other person has it. Also, their efforts in this regard will not be desperate. They will neither try to spoil things for the other person in action or thought nor will they devalue the other person in their mind or to others.

- When a self-devaluation attitude is a prominent feature of unhealthy envy, I discuss the importance of developing an attitude of unconditional self-acceptance as a solution.

- Yet again, if the person is interested, I will help them change their rigid/extreme attitudes to their flexible/non-extreme counterparts and help them think and act in ways that will support the development of these attitudes.

30. Helping the Client to Understand and Deal with Procrastination

Sometimes people seek ONEplus therapy for help with procrastination. I have found it useful to do the following.

- It is important that my client and I agree with one another concerning what we mean by procrastination. I thus ask the person what they mean by procrastination. I also ask them if they are interested in my definition which is 'putting off a task that is in your interest to do and putting it off beyond the time when it's in your interest to do it' (Dryden, 2012: 267).

- Once we have agreed on what procrastination is, we need to be clear with one another if procrastination is a problem for the person and if so, how would they like to change and why they would like to see this change in their life.

- In doing the above, it is worth spending some time doing a cost-benefit analysis on procrastination and whatever change the person nominates. I am particularly interested in helping the person articulate what benefits they derive from procrastination and what costs they think they will experience if they strive for what they consider the healthy alternative to procrastination.

- In doing this, I focus on the values they have as a person that underpin the healthy alternative and how procrastination goes against these values.

- When a self-devaluation attitude is a prominent feature of procrastination, I discuss the importance of developing an attitude of unconditional self-acceptance as a solution.

- When an attitude of unbearability is a prominent feature of procrastination, I discuss the importance of developing an attitude of bearability as a solution.

I also share with them, if they are interested, the following ideas:

- It is useful to ask yourself what conditions you think need to be in place before you commence the task you have been procrastinating on. The following are the frequently mentioned conditions:

  - Motivation (see the section above entitled, 'Helping the Client Distinguish Between Enthusiasm-Based Motivation, Fear-based Motivation and Reason-Based Motivation)

- Comfort
- Confidence
- A sense of competence that I can do the task
- Certainty that I will be successful at the task
- Immediate understanding
- Being in the mood to do the task
- Pressure
- Fear
- Enjoyment
- Having done all the preparations

- Once you have identified the condition(s) that you think you need to be in place before you commence the task, ask yourself whether it is possible for you to begin the task without the presence of your 'needed' condition(s).

- Once I have helped the person see that their specified conditions are desirable but not necessary, I say the following: Imagine yourself doing the task without the (now) desired condition while reminding yourself of the reasons why you are doing the task now and the values that underpin you choosing to do it. Can you imagine yourself doing it? How does it feel to see yourself do it?

- If they find this a useful task, then it forms part of the solution that they are looking for.

- Yet again, if the person is interested, I will help them change their rigid/extreme attitudes to their flexible/non-extreme counterparts and help them think and act in ways that will support the development of these attitudes.

This brings us to the end of the book. If you have any feedback I would be pleased to receive it at windy@windydryden.com

Appendix 1

The Conventional Therapy Mindset

- Therapy is likely to take time to yield a benefit for clients.

- It is vital to provide ongoing therapy for some clients and an agreed number of sessions for others. The purpose of the first session is to help the therapist to determine which mode of therapy is suitable for which client.

- The more complex and severe the client's problems, the longer they will need to be in therapy.

- Many clients benefit from having a relationship of depth with their therapists. Such a relationship takes a while to develop, and in some cases, it will take months or years.

- Clients generally need time to get used to being in therapy.

- Clients need to talk about whatever they wish, particularly at the beginning, and therapists should allow them to do this.

- The early phase of therapy should be taken up with assessing the client, taking a case history and developing a case formulation.

- The purpose of the first psychotherapy session is to encourage the client to come back for a second.

- A client's problems will be resolved when they have worked through these via the transference. This requires time.

- Clients need to learn new skills from therapy; this takes time.

- Empirically supported treatments require multiple sessions.

- A client's initial *presenting* problems are not as significant as their real problems, which they will take time to reveal.

Appendix 2

What is ONEplus Therapy
Information for Prospective Clients
Windy Dryden PhD[45]

- ONEplus Therapy is an intentional endeavour where you and I set out with the purpose of helping you in one session, on the understanding that more help is available to you if you want it.

- At the end of the session, we will agree on a way forward. Thus, (i) you may decide to seek no further help; (ii) you may decide to reflect on and digest what you learned in the session, act on what you learned and see what happens before deciding whether to seek further help; or iii) you may decide to arrange for further help at the end of the session. If the latter, we can discuss what further help is available so you can choose what best suits you. Each of these ways forward is equally OK.

- ONEplus Therapy is based on offering help at the point of need rather than at the point of availability. It has the effect of you being seen quickly when you need help

- ONEplus Therapy is based on three foundations:

    - The most frequent number of sessions clients have internationally is '1', followed by '2', '3', and so on.

---

[45] Enquiries about being a client in ONEplus Therapy should be directed to Professor Windy Dryden on 07971 214196 or at windy@windydryden.com

- 70–80% of those who have one session are satisfied with that session, given their current circumstances.
- Therapists are poor at predicting who will attend only one session and who will attend more.

- My primary goal in ONEplus Therapy is to provide you with the help YOU want. This may include my:

  - Helping you to address a specific issue with which you are stuck. Here I will help you to take a few steps forward, which may encourage you to travel the rest of the journey without my professional assistance.
  - Helping you to get a greater understanding of an issue
  - Helping you to express your feelings about an issue.
  - Helping you to make a decision or resolve a dilemma.

- People have found it helpful to prepare for the session so that they can get the most from it. To this end, I will send you a questionnaire to complete and return. This is NOT compulsory, but it helps us both prepare for the session.

- The focus of a session in ONEplus Therapy is on us negotiating a goal for that session. If you have a specific issue that you wish to address, I will help you to find and rehearse a solution that facilitates the achievement of this goal. Then, I will help you to devise an action plan which you can implement after the session.

- In ONEplus Therapy, I will help you to:

  - Discover what you have done in the past to deal with your problem. I will then encourage you to use what has been helpful and set aside what has not been helpful.
  - Identify and use your internal strengths and external resources in implementing the agreed solution.

- I encourage follow-up to discover how you are getting on and to improve service delivery, and at the end of the session, we will make an appointment for a follow-up, but only if you wish.

Appendix 3

ONEplus Therapy Skills Evaluation Form

NAME: **DATE:**

SKILL AREA For each item, mark '✓', 'x' or 'n/a'	Session
Developed the working alliance at the outset and maintained it throughout	
Was clear with the client concerning the purpose of the session and what can and cannot be achieved	
Asked the client how they thought they could best be helped and gave them some alternatives when necessary	
Elicited the client's goal for the session, rather than from therapy	
Asked what the client is prepared to sacrifice to achieve their goal	
Was focused and encouraged the client to stay focused	
Elicited and understood the problem from the client's perspective	

SKILL AREA For each item, mark '✔', 'x' or 'n/a'	Session
Assessed the client's nominated problem	
Bridged to the future whenever possible	
Used questions constructively - Ensured that the client answered the questions they were asked - Gave the client time to answer questions	
Clarity - Whenever practicable, gave an explanation for interventions made, but did not do so obsessively - Checked out the client's understanding of substantive points	
Encouraged the client to be as specific as possible but was mindful of opportunities for generalisation	
Identified and encouraged the client to use internal strengths	
Identified and encouraged the client to use external resources	

SKILL AREA For each item, mark '✓', 'x' or 'n/a'	Session
Identified the client's previous attempts to solve their problem - Encouraged the client to capitalise on successful attempts - Discouraged the client from using unsuccessful attempts	
Undertook solution-focused work	
Offered the client expertise without assuming the role of expert	
Looked for ways of making an emotional impact without pushing for it	
Encouraged the client to select a solution that they were most likely to implement	
Encouraged the client to rehearse the solution in the session	
Encouraged the client to take away just one thing from the session	
Had the client summarise the session rather than summarising for the client	
Helped the client to develop an action plan	

SKILL AREA For each item, mark '✓', 'x' or 'n/a'	Session
Encouraged the client to identify and problem-solve potential obstacles	
Identified and responded to the client's doubts, reservations and objections	
Tied-up any loose ends: - Reminded the client of how they may access future help - Explained the 'reflect-digest-act-wait-decide' process - Invited the client to ask any last-minute questions - Invited the client to tell the counsellor something that they needed to say before the close of the session	
Sought feedback from the client	

215

RATE PARTICIPANT 1 TO 5 *(see scale at bottom):*	
Overall performance in the session	
General knowledge of ONEplus therapy	
Potential for skill in ONEplus therapy	
COMMON ERRORS:	
Too passive	
Too much lecturing	
Let the client discuss their problem in too much detail when not requested	
Not sufficiently goal focused	
SUPERVISOR'S INITIALS:	

✓ - Adequately demonstrated skill
x - Failed to demonstrate skill
n/a - Not appropriate

1 - Excellent, outstanding (top 10% overall of course participants)
2 - Good, above average, satisfactory
3 - Fair, average, but still satisfactory
4 - Poor, needs to demonstrate improved skills
5 - Inadequate, Fail (should not be awarded the certificate unless redeemed on subsequent assessment)

NB. If the majority of the student's ratings are 'x' meaning that they failed to demonstrate a relevant skill, then their overall performance will be rated as '5' (inadequate) and they are deemed to have failed the assessment. They will not be awarded the certificate unless they pass at re-assessment.

Appendix 4

What is ONEplus Therapy?
Information for Stakeholders
Windy Dryden PhD[46]

- ONEplus Therapy is an intentional endeavour where both parties set out with the purpose of helping the client in one session, on the understanding that more help is available to the client if they want it.

- At the end of the session, I will agree on a way forward with the client. Thus, they may decide (i) to seek no further help; (ii) to reflect on and digest what they learned in the session, act on what they learned and see what happens before deciding whether to seek further help; or (iii) to arrange for further help at the end of the session. If the latter, the client and I discuss what further help is available so they can choose what best suits them. I stress to the client that these ways forward are equally OK.

- ONEplus Therapy is based on offering help at the point of need rather than at the point of availability. It has the effect of reducing waiting lists.

- ONEplus Therapy is based on three foundations:

---

[46] For further information about ONEplus Therapy and to refer clients, contact Professor Windy Dryden on 07971 214196 or at windy@windydryden.com

- The most frequent number of sessions clients have internationally is '1', followed by '2', '3', and so on.
- 70–80% of those who have one session are satisfied with that session, given their current circumstances.
- Therapists are poor at predicting who will attend only one session and who will attend more.

• My primary goal in ONEplus Therapy is to provide the client with the help THEY want. This may include me:

- Helping them to address a specific issue with which they are stuck. Here I will help them to take a few steps forward, which may encourage them to travel the rest of the journey without my professional assistance.
- Helping them to get a greater understanding of an issue.
- Helping them to express their feelings about an issue.
- Helping them to make a decision or resolve a dilemma.

• Clients have found it helpful to prepare for the session so that they can get the most from it. To this end, I will send the client a questionnaire to complete and return. This is NOT compulsory, but it helps both the client and me to prepare for the session.

• A session in ONEplus Therapy focuses on negotiating a goal for that session with the client. If they have a specific issue that they wish to address, I will help them to find and rehearse a solution that facilitates the achievement of this goal. Then, I will help them devise an action plan they can implement after the session.

- In ONEplus Therapy, I will help the client to:

  - Discover what they have done in the past to deal
    with their problem. I will then encourage them to
    use what has been helpful and set aside what has not
    been helpful.
  - Identify and use their internal strengths and external
    resources in implementing the agreed solution.

- Follow-up is encouraged to discover how the client is
  getting on and to improve service delivery.

Appendix 5

Introduction Email and Invitation to Complete a Pre-Session Questionnaire

Dear John,

We have a 30-minute counselling session booked through Fortune Health on _____, and I look forward to meeting you.

I have found it useful to ask clients to prepare for their session with me, and to that effect, I would be grateful if you would download and complete the attached form. Let me emphasise that this is not mandatory; just something that will help you get the most from our session. If you decide to complete it, I would be grateful if you would share a copy with me by email attachment so I can prepare for our session too.

Please be in an indoor, private space with no disruptions and a good internet connection. It does not work to have a counselling session in a coffee bar, in a car (even when stationary) or in an outside space.

Best wishes,

Windy Dryden

Appendix 6

Pre-session Telephone Protocol

Name: **Date:**

What made you decide that now is the right time for therapy?	
How do you anticipate the issue could be solved?	
How soon do you think the issue could be solved?	
How can I best help you to deal with the issue?	
What are the factors (or circumstances) that have contributed to the issue?	

What have you tried to do that has helped with the issue?	
What have you tried that has not helped with the issue?	
What core values do you have that we might refer to in our work together in addressing your problem?	
What strengths do you have as a person that you can use that might help you address the issue?	
Can you tell me about an occasion where you made a significant change in outlook in a very short period of time.	

Who do you consider to be a role model who might directly or indirectly be helpful to you as you deal with the problem?	
I would like to know what your preferred way of learning is so that I can tailor the session to best help you. Can you help shed light on this?	
Between now and our face-to face-session, I want you to notice the things that happen to you that you would like to keep happening in the future relevant to the problem. In this way, you will help me to find out more about your goal.	

Is there anything that you would like me to know that will help me prepare for our face-to-face session or that would help us get the most out of the session?	

Appendix 7

Pre-Session Preparation Questionnaire

Pre-Session Questionnaire

I invite you to fill in this questionnaire before your session with me. This will help you to prepare for the session so that you can get the most from it. It also helps me to help you as effectively as I can. Please return it by email attachment before our session. Please be brief and concise in your answers.

Name:
Date:

1. **What is the issue that you want to focus on in the session?**
   Be concise. In one or two sentences get to the heart of the problem, if possible.

   ```



   ```

2. **Why is this significant?**
   What's at stake? How does this affect your life? What is the future impact if the issue is not resolved?

   ```



   ```

3.   What do you want to get from the session?

```

```

4.   Specify briefly the relevant background information.
What you think I need to know about the issue to help you with it? Summarise in bullet points.

```

```

5.   How have you tried to deal with the issue up to this point?
What steps, successful or unsuccessful have you taken so far in addressing the issue?

```

```

6.   What are the strengths or inner resources that you have as a person that you could draw upon while tackling the issue?
If you struggle with answering this question, think of what people who really know you and who are on your side would say.

```

```

7. **Who are the people in your life who can support you as you tackle the issue?**
   Name them and say what help each can provide.

8. **What help do you hope I can best provide you in the session? Please check the main <u>one</u>.**

   □ Help me to develop greater understanding of the issue

   □ Just listen while I talk about the issue

   □ Help me to express my feelings about the issue

   □ Help me to solve an emotional or behavioural problem; help me get unstuck

   □ Help me to make a decision

   □ Help me to resolve a dilemma

   □ Other (please specify):

Thank you.
Windy Dryden

Appendix 8

ONEplus Therapy Notes

Name:
Date of therapy session:

Help requested by client (list the main one)
- ☐ To develop greater understanding of the issue
- ☐ For me to listen while they talk about the issue
- ☐ To express their feelings about the issue
- ☐ To solve an emotional or behavioural problem; to get unstuck
- ☐ To make a decision
- ☐ To resolve a dilemma
- ☐ To request a professional opinion on something
- ☐ To discuss what help they need about an issue (i.e.signposting)
- ☐ Other:

Client's goal for the session:

Agreed focus:

Highlights of the session:

Client takeaway(s):

What was agreed about the client accessing further help:

- ☐ The client will make contact again if they need further help
- ☐ The client will reflect, digest, take action, let time pass and make contact if they need further help (agreed time period is _____)
- ☐ An appointment for further help was agreed at the end of the session
- ☐ I agreed to contact the person at an agreed time to see if further help is needed (agreed time period is _____)
- ☐ Other:

Appendix 9

ONEplus Therapy Session Rating Scale [OTSRS]

Name:
Date:

It is very important for me to monitor my counselling work. So, please rate the session you recently had with me by <u>underlining</u> the number that best fits your experience on the following scales.

The pre-session questionnaire was not useful in helping me to prepare for the session	0 1 2 3 4 5 6 7 8 9 10	The pre-session questionnaire was useful in helping me to prepare for the session
I did not feel heard, understood or respected by Windy Dryden in the session	0 1 2 3 4 5 6 7 8 9 10	I did feel heard, understood and respected by Windy Dryden in the session
Windy Dryden and I did not discuss what I I wanted to discuss in the session	0 1 2 3 4 5 6 7 8 9 10	Windy Dryden and I did discuss what I wanted to discuss in the session
Windy Dryden's approach was not a good fit for me	0 1 2 3 4 5 6 7 8 9 10	Windy Dryden's approach was a good fit for me
Overall, I did not get what I wanted from my session with Windy Dryden	0 1 2 3 4 5 6 7 8 9 10	Overall, I did get what I wanted from my session with Windy Dryden

If I wanted another counselling session, I would not choose Windy Dryden as my counsellor   **0 1 2 3 4 5 6 7 8 9 10**   If I wanted another counselling session, I would choose Windy Dryden as my counsellor

Finally, if there was anything that was particularly useful or anything I could have done to have improved the session for you, please let me know in the box below:

Thank you for your feedback. Please email this form back to

_____

Appendix 10

Follow-Up Telephone Evaluation Protocol

1. Check that the client has the time to talk now (i.e., approximately 20–30 minutes)? Are they able and willing to talk freely, privately and in confidence?

    Client Response:

2. Read to the client verbatim their original statement of the problem, issue, obstacle or complaint. Ask: 'Do you recall that?' 'Is that accurate?'

    Client Response:

3. Would you say that the issue (re-state as described by the client) is about the same or has changed? If changed, list five-point scale as follows:

    (1)------------(2)------------(3)------------ (4)------------ (5)

    Much worse   About the same   Much improved

    Client Response:

4. What do you think made the change (for better or worse) possible. If conditions are the same, ask 'What makes it stay the same?'

Client Response:

5. If people around you give you the feedback that you have changed, how do they think you have changed?

Client Response:

6. Besides the specific issue of…. (state the problem), have there been other areas that have changed (for better or worse). If so what?

Client Response:

7. Now please let me ask you a few questions about the therapy that you received. What do you recall from that session?

Client Response:

8. What do you recall that was particularly helpful or unhelpful?

    Client Response:

9. How have you been able to make use of the session recording if at all? If so, what was helpful about it?

    Client Response:

10. If you received a written transcript of the session, what use did you make of it?

    Client Response:

11. How satisfied are you with the therapy that you received? Ask the client to make their ration on the five-point scale as follows and ask them to explain their rating

    (1)-------------(2)--------------(3)-------------(4)-------------(5)

    Very   Neither Satisfied   Very
    Dissatisfied   Nor Dissatisfied   Satisfied

    Client Response:

12. Did you find the single session to be sufficient? If not, would you wish to resume therapy? Would you wish to change therapist?

Client Response:

13. If you had any recommendations for improvement in the service that you received, what would they be?

Client Response:

14. Is there anything else I have not specifically asked you that you would like me to know?

Client Response:

Thank the client for their time and participation. Remind them that they can contact you or the agency again if they need further help.

References

Beck, A.T., Epstein, N., & Harrison, R. (1983). Cognitions, attitudes and personality dimensions in depression. *British Journal of Cognitive Psychotherapy 1*(1), 1–16.

Bennett, R., & Oliver, J.E. (2019). *Acceptance and Commitment Therapy: 100 Key Points and Techniques.* Abingdon, Oxon: Routledge.

Bloom, B.L. (1981). Focused single-session therapy: Initial development and evaluation. In S. Budman (ed.), *Forms of Brief Therapy* (pp. 167–216). New York: Guilford Press.

Bloom, B.L. (1992). *Planned Short-Term Psychotherapy: A Clinical Handbook.* Boston, MA: Allyn and Bacon.

Bordin, E.S. (1979). The generalizability of the psychoanalytic concept of the working alliance. *Psychotherapy: Theory, Research and Practice 16*, 252–260.

Brown, G.S., & Jones, E.R. (2005). Implementing a feedback system in a managed care environment: What are patients teaching us? *Journal of Clinical Psychology 61,* 187–198.

Cannistrà, F. (2022). The single session therapy mindset: Fourteen principles gained through an analysis of the literature. *International Journal of Brief Therapy and Family Science 12* (1), 1–26.

Colman, A. (2015). *Oxford Dictionary of Psychology.* 4th edn. Oxford: Oxford University Press.

Cooper, M. & McLeod, J. (2011). *Pluralistic Counselling and Psychotherapy.* London: Sage.

Dryden, W. (2011). *Counselling in a Nutshell.* 2nd edition. London: Sage.

Dryden, W. (2012). Dealing with procrastination: The REBT approach and a demonstration session. *Journal of Rational-Emotive & Cognitive-Behavior Therapy 30*, 264–281.

Dryden, W. (2016). *Attitudes in Rational Emotive Behaviour Therapy: Components, Characteristics and Adversity-Related Consequences.* London: Rationality Publications.

Dryden, W. (2021). *Seven Principles of Doing Live Therapy Demonstrations.* London: Rationality Publications.

Dryden, W. (2022a). *Single-Session Therapy: Responses to Frequently Asked Questions.* Abingdon, Oxon: Routledge.

Dryden, W. (2022b). *Single-Session Integrated CBT (SSI-CBT): Distinctive Features. 2nd edition.* Abingdon, Oxon: Routledge.

Dryden, W. (2022c). *The Rational Emotive Behaviour Therapy Primer: A Concise Introduction.* Monmouth: PCCS Books.

Dryden, W. (2023). *Single-Session Therapy and Regret.* Sheffield: Onlinevents Publications.

Dryden, W. (2024). *Single-Session Therapy: 100 Key Points and Techniques.* 2nd edition. Abingdon, Oxon: Routledge.

Ellis, A. (1977). Fun as psychotherapy, *Rational Living 12*(1), 2–6.

Ellis, A. (1994). *Reason and Emotion in Psychotherapy.* Revised and Expanded Edition. New York: Birch Lane Press.

Frank, J.D. (1961). *Persuasion and Healing: A Comprehensive Study of Psychotherapy.* Baltimore, MD: The Johns Hopkins Press.

Freud, S. & Breuer, J. (1895). *Studien Über Hysterie.* Leipzig and Vienna: Deuticke.

Hoyt, M. F. (2011). Foreword. In A. Slive & M. Bobele (eds). (2011). *When One Hour Is All You Have: Effective Therapy for Walk-in Clients* (pp. xix–xv). Phoenix, AZ: Zeig, Tucker & Theisen.

Hoyt, M. F. & Talmon, M. (eds). (2014). *Capturing the Moment: Single Session Therapy and Walk-in Services.* Bethel, CT: Crown House Publishing Ltd.

Hoyt, M.F., Rosenbaum, R. & Talmon, M. (1992). Planned single-session psychotherapy. In S.H. Budman, M.F. Hoyt, & S. Friedman (eds), *The First Session in Brief Therapy* (pp. 59–86). New York: Guilford Press.

Hoyt, M.F., Bobele, M., Slive, A., Young, J. & Talmon, M. (eds). (2018). *Single-Session Therapy by Walk-In or Appointment: Administrative, Clinical, and Supervisory Aspects of One-at-a-Time Services.* New York: Routledge.

Hoyt, M.F., Young, J., & Rycroft, P (eds). (2021). *Single Session Thinking and Practice in Global, Cultural and Familial Contexts: Expanding Applications.* New York: Routledge.

Kuehn, J.L. (1965). Encounter at Leyden: Gustav Mahler consults Sigmund Freud. *Psychoanalytic Review 52*, 345–364.

Lemma, A. (2000). *Humour on the Couch: Exploring Humour in Psychotherapy and in Everyday Life.* London: Whurr.

Miller, W.R. & C' de Baca, J. (2001). *Quantum Change: When Epiphanies and Sudden Insights Transform Ordinary Lives.* New York: Guilford.

Norcross, J.C., & Cooper, M. (2021). *Personalizing Psychotherapy: Assessing and Accommodating Patient Preferences.* Washington, DC: American Psychological Association.

Rycroft, P. (2018). Capturing the moment in supervision. In M.F. Hoyt, M. Bobele, A. Slive, J. Young, & M. Talmon (eds), *Single-Session Therapy by Walk-In or Appointment: Administrative, Clinical, and Supervisory Aspects of One-at-a-Time Services* (pp. 347–365). New York: Routledge.

Rycroft, P., & Young, J. (2021). Translating single session thinking into practice. In M.F. Hoyt, J. Young & P. Rycroft (eds), *Single Session Thinking and Practice in Global, Cultural and Familial Contexts: Expanding Applications* (pp. 42–53). New York: Routledge.

Seabury, B.A., Seabury, B.H., & Garvin, C.D. (2011). *Foundations of Interpersonal Practice in Social Work: Promoting Competence in Generalist Practice.* 3rd ed. Thousand Oaks, CA: Sage Publications.

Schleider, J.L., Dobias, M.L., Sung, J.Y., & Mullarkey M.C. (2020). Future directions in single-session youth mental health interventions. *Journal of Clinical Child and Adolescent Psychology 2*, 264–278.

Sharoff, K. (2002). *Cognitive Coping Therapy*. New York: Brunner-Mazel.

Shostrom, E.L. (Producer). (1965). *Three Approaches to Psychotherapy, Series I* [*Motion picture*]. (Available from Psychological & Educational Films, 3334 East Coast Highway #252, Corona Del Mar, CA 92625).

Simon, G.E., Imel, Z.E., Ludman, E.J. & Steinfeld, B.J. (2012). Is dropout after a first psychotherapy visit always a bad outcome? *Psychiatric Services 63*(7), 705–707.

Slive, A. & Bobele, M. (eds). (2011). *When One Hour Is All You Have: Effective Therapy for Walk-in Clients*. Phoenix, AZ: Zeig, Tucker & Theisen.

Slive, A., McElheran, N., & Lawson, A. (2008). How brief does it get? Walk-in single-session therapy. *Journal of Systemic Therapies 27*, 5–22.

Söderquist, M. (2023). *Single Session One at a Time Counselling with Couples: Challenge and Possibility*. Abingdon, Oxon: Routledge.

Spoerl, O.H. (1975). Single session-psychotherapy. *Diseases of the Nervous System 36*(6), 283–285.

Swaminath, G. (2006). Joke's a part: In defence of humour. *Indian Journal of Psychiatry 48*(3), 177–180.

Talmon, M. (1990). *Single Session Therapy: Maximising the Effect of the First (and Often Only) Therapeutic Encounter*. San Francisco: Jossey-Bass.

Young, J. (2018). SST: The misunderstood gift that keeps on giving. In M.F. Hoyt, M. Bobele, A. Slive, J. Young, & M. Talmon (eds), *Single-Session Therapy by Walk-In or Appointment: Administrative, Clinical, and Supervisory Aspects of One-at-a-Time Services* (pp. 40–58). New York: Routledge.

Index

241